ANOTHER JOURNEY
THROUGH BRITAIN

MARK PROBERT

MGP PUBLISHING

'FEELING GOOD'

Written by Leslie Bricusse and Anthony Newley

Concord Music Ltd of Suite 2.07, Plaza 535 Kings Road, London, SW10 0SZ

International Copyright Secured, All Rights Reserved. Used with Permission.

ISBN 9781916305601

Disclaimer

This book depicts events in the author's life as truthfully as recollection permits, which he readily admits, becomes increasingly vague as the years go by. It is not intended to be an academic text; it aims to entertain, and to some extent, inform. Apart from descriptions and opinions provided by the author, this book includes information derived from many sources, including Internet research. The information represented is believed to be correct, but that is only valid if the source and its interpretation are also correct. The publisher apologises for any errors or omissions and would be grateful to be notified of any suggestions for correction to improve the quality of future reprints or editions of this book (please send comments to mgprobert.com). Occasionally, dialogue consistent with the character or nature of the person speaking has been supplemented. Some names, places, and identifying details have been changed to protect the privacy of individuals.

To Jan

CONTENTS

ILLUSTRATIONS

ANOTHER JOURNEY THROUGH BRITAIN

BEFORE THE JOURNEY

The visitor centre car park at Land's End was almost empty and ghostly silent. It was just after 10 am on a chilly May morning. The sun was up there somewhere, trying to find its way through a thin layer of hazy clouds. I parked my Royal Enfield motorcycle and switched the engine off. Standing beside the bike, I was quietly surveying the surrounding scene before dashing into a souvenir shop to get a tacky sticker to put on my bike's windscreen. I'm not a big fan of what to me has become a distasteful blot on an otherwise beautiful Cornish landscape – but needs must, and a guy has to have a tacky sticker.

An unkempt silver Volvo estate car rattled its way towards me, disturbing the stillness of the morning as it scrunched across the gravel. Despite having the choice of what looked like at least a hundred empty spaces to choose from, it ended up right next to me. Why do people do that?

I witnessed an emergency escape drill. The car doors exploded open and Mum, Dad and three hyperactive offspring burst out into what had been a peaceful car park. The kids were in the five- to eight-year-old age range, and they ran around like they'd overdosed on high-caffeine energy drinks. Dad managed a brief nod in my direction but in a flash the family had slammed the doors shut again and raced off towards the Land's End sensory cinema experience.

What's wrong with those guys? Why can't they take a walk along the clifftops and soak up the natural peace and beauty of the place?

Anyway, in the few seconds while their car doors were open, a musical blast had escaped, to further shatter the serenity of the morning – Pink Floyd, on maximum volume, and with cash register accompaniment, blasting out a few lines of 'Money'. An excellent choice – maybe I'll let them off. The tension I sensed as the Volvo first parked next to me fell away. I had to smile as I caught that brief burst of iconic music greatness. I smiled inwardly; it was going to be a good day.

My internal jukebox took over; that song would now be on a continuous loop for several hours. As Dave Gilmour resumed the vocals in my head, my thoughts skipped quickly from how 'it's a gas' seemed such an outdated thing to say, to the rarity of a 7/4 time signature in popular music. I didn't dwell on it. Standing there quietly amused, I watched the thrill-seekers disappear in search of stimulation before uttering a quiet 'fair play' under my breath in admiration of Mum and Dad's good taste in music.

How appropriate those 'Money' lyrics seemed for the Land's End pleasure park. I began to compose headlines for the day's travel blog (which sadly no longer exists) in my head. 'The Last Resort', 'Land's Spend' and 'Unhappy End' were all contenders. I had no problem thinking of colourful words to describe how that magnificent headland had been turned into what I saw as an over-commercialised tourist trap.

But then I thought, wait a second – if I was an eight-year-old *Wallace & Gromit* fan, or a parent looking for something to hold a kid's attention for an hour, I might see things differently. You pays your money...

Anyway, I was there now; I just had to dash in, buy that

sticker and get on my way. Pink Floyd's 'Money' continued to play in my head. It was enough of a distraction to avoid thinking about the irony of my trinket raid. I undoubtedly was in the right.

That song took me back in time, the way songs do, to when I first heard it. I was a nineteen-year-old again, at college in Kent in 1973. All flares and denim.

It's magic, isn't it? You catch part of a song or tune from the past, and you're spirited back to that first time. If I hear 'Happy Talk' from *South Pacific*, I can still see the old Bush stereogram in our 1960s lounge, when I was about eight. The Beatle's 'She's Leaving Home' whisks me back to a steam-driven fairground as a thirteen-year-old, and The Beach Boys' 'Good Vibrations' is a sweltering day on the beach at Newquay as a teenager. I can sense the warm sand under my feet, squeezing between my toes. I only have to hear a handful of notes from 'I'm Not In Love' by 10cc, and I'm twenty again, in my first car, a little lime-green Mini, pulled over to the side of the road in Moseley, Birmingham, with the radio turned up to the max. I'm there… it's May 1975 and I've just left home to live in a strange unknown city. I can smell the mustiness of the damp gutters that loosely held the car's sliding windows. I've got that nervous excitement of leaving home, starting a fresh job, with places to go, things to do, girls to meet… and I wasn't in love.

Everyone knows that feeling of being transported back in time. You're thinking of your examples right now. The phenomenon even has a scientific acronym – MEAM, or Music Evoked Autobiographical Memory. As our neural networks develop, they somehow associate life experiences with the music of the moment. You hear the music and retrieve the associated memory. There must be some evolutionary explanation, but I don't know what it is. And it's not just music. Fond memories and feelings come flooding back when I catch a whiff of mown grass or two-stroke engine

3

exhaust. The memories associated with the smell of baby sick are more mixed.

Book quotes can have the same effect. No really, stay with me on this. It's known as Literary Evoked Autobiographical Memory – LEAM. Well, it is now because I just made it up. I can read a few lines from a book and I'm transported to when I first read them, to the time, the place and my feelings.

The opening lines of John Hillaby's *Journey through Britain*, published in 1968, describe an incident that happened a few weeks into his epic walk. He's in a forest somewhere along the border between England and Wales... and he's lost. Whenever I read the opening lines, I'm a fifteen-year-old lad in Kent, reading the book for the first time, shortly after it had been published. Our family had moved to a new house, I was attending my third secondary school in four years, and to put it mildly, I wasn't very happy about it.

John Hillaby was a travel writer and naturalist who was once described as 'the most celebrated pedestrian in England'. He wrote a series of books describing his long-distance walks in Africa and Europe. *Journey through Britain* was published to critical acclaim, with one reviewer stating that it 'may prove to be a classic in travel literature'. The book told the story of John Hillaby's 1,100-mile walk from Land's End to John o' Groats, and it captured my imagination. It was my escape – just what I needed. For me, at that moment, the book was perfect. As I read it, I walked every step with John; I happily took the blisters for a few hours of release from my real-world anxieties. The text jumped with effortless dexterity from factual description to social commentary to amusing anecdote. By today's standards, the style seems a little formal and dated, and it is. The book is fifty years old, but it has a gentle flow and reading a chapter or two always brings a smile to my face. For those of you interested to read more about John, I've included a short biography at the end of this book.

I picked up *Journey through Britain* again in 2010 after

undertaking a similar journey myself. When I say similar, in reality it was nothing like it. I didn't even walk. I rode a comfortable touring bicycle and had the luxury of a motorhome to sleep in most nights. As I went through the book a second time, it intrigued me how much some things had changed since John Hillaby's days, while other things hadn't altered at all. The pre-history and geology aren't any different, but many of the places and much of the culture he described have changed dramatically in fifty years. I enjoyed reading, for example, how he came across the M4 being constructed across the Severn Estuary. That scene is hard to imagine now after fifty years of bridge tolls and being able to dash eastwards along the M4 to escape the Welsh rain. The changes in social attitudes are even more striking. By today's social norms, it's amusing to read about the 'beatniks' in Newquay and the local fisherman's indignation at seeing a young girl bathing naked at dusk. If there are any fishermen left in Newquay today their small talk over net-mending duties is more likely to involve the town's ban on stag parties and blow-up sex toys, and the effect on tourist numbers.

I read the book again in 2018, as I was entering semi-retirement. Bits and pieces of work allowed me to keep scratching my travel itch, but the proportion of my time spent working was falling away. After over forty years of work, I was lifting my head to see what was happening around me. Retirement was looming. Now what? It occurred to me that it would be a bit of a wheeze to repeat John Hillaby's journey, looking out for the things he wrote about in his original book. I could see how today's Britain differed from the country he observed fifty years ago. Do those rich local dialects, so colourfully described by the author, still exist, and are they so regionally defined? How has the economic landscape changed, and how have people's attitudes changed? Do the public houses still exist in the same numbers, and would I still find such colourful characters in them? Brilliant; I'd be able to visit as many pubs as I wanted to, and it would be research!

Social media is a mixed blessing. The more time I had to engage with it, the more I came across sad stories of ex-work colleagues suffering from serious illnesses, or even worse. It made me think. Without being morbid, I needed to make the most of whatever time I'd got left. As with many of the baby boomer generation, I was fortunate to have some time, and the means, to do something other than work. More family time was a big bonus but retracing the footsteps of John Hillaby and observing the changes along his route was just the excuse I needed for an adventure. As a bonus, I could postpone that list of jobs around the house a while longer.

I started my planning. Asking my wife for a three-month pass to traipse the length of Britain seemed unreasonable. That was an honourable way out, because I don't suppose I could manage the walk, anyway. Maybe I could do it by bicycle over six leisurely weeks? I'd need time to get to the start and get home again though, so it could end up taking the best part of two months. I didn't have that much time either. Looking for a solution, I next considered doing the trip by motorbike. Yes! That would be just as much fun and I could do it all in three weeks. At a nice slow pace, I'd still be able to smell the fields and be immersed in the landscape. Not as much as John Hillaby, because he stuck to the footpaths and tracks for his route, but close enough. OK then, it seemed a reasonable compromise; time to get back to the planning.

The outline for an adventure was taking shape. It would be a three-week motorcycle ride from Land's End to John o' Groats, sticking as closely as possible to the original 1966 route. I'd take it easy and note the changes that had occurred throughout Great Britain in fifty years. I made my choice of mount – a Royal Enfield Classic 500. The design of the bike is straight out of the 1950s. It wouldn't have been out of place in the landscape that John Hillaby passed through on his epic walk. Even at that early stage of planning, the possibility of a book came to mind, and I started thinking of titles. As I would be setting off from Cornwall, I flirted, but for less than a second, with the title 'Zennor and the art of motorcycle maintenance'.

I felt a bit of a fraud. I was tackling a repeat of an epic walking journey by motorbike. It still seemed like a wonderful excuse for an adventure though. I thought of my expedition as being a motorcycling version of Michael Portillo's review of the 1866 *Bradshaw's Railway Guide* – but without the pastel jackets – or the trains.

By using a motorcycle, there was a danger that I'd go past everything too quickly; a walker has time to observe so much more. To mitigate this, I'd limit my rides to around a hundred miles a day and make a point of frequent stops and diversions. I would slow my pace of travel right down and take time to explore places, see the things that define each region I passed through, and meet its people. By taking my time over the journey, I reckoned I could pace my schedule to cover one of the original *Journey through Britain* chapters each day – around 15 days for my version, with a few days extra to get there and back. My only real constraint was not being able to follow the paths, but I'd keep my route as close as possible to the original one and go to most of the same places, taking the occasional walk along those same paths.

Land's End to John o' Groats (often referred to as LeJog) is an iconic journey, done so many times and in so many ways. In some respects, it's a bit of a marketing coup, or at least a terrific bit of opportunism by the people living in those two places. The terminals are neither the most southerly nor the most northerly points on the British mainland. Those are the Lizard and Dunnet Head. Although Land's End can claim to be the most south-westerly extremity, the opposite diagonal corner is near to Duncansby Head, a further five miles northeast from John o' Groats. One definition of the Land's End to John o' Groats route is that it's the longest journey between two inhabited points on the British mainland, traditionally accepted as being 874 miles. Whatever – the route has now become established and thousands of people attempt it each year. It's been done on a motorbike in a face-melting and barely believable time of just over 11 hours. You name it, and someone has completed the journey with it – skateboard, wheelchair, bed, JCB digger, lawnmower, unicycle, bus and many other means.

In writing about my trip, I've kept to the same overall structure as the original book. I follow this opening introductory chapter with sections of the journey that broadly match those used by John Hillaby. In each chapter, I have described my journey and the things that occurred along the way. I've also looked at aspects of modern culture and society and tried to make some comparisons over time.

It would be impossible to follow John Hillaby's exact route all the way, but within the restrictions already mentioned, the tracks of our two journeys are very similar. After surfing up the north coast of Cornwall, my route headed eastwards and inland to squelch across Dartmoor. It then crossed the Somerset lowlands, headed for Bristol and turned the corner into Wales shortly after crossing the Severn Estuary. The route then sheepishly skirted the Welsh/English border for a while before turning further inland towards Stoke and the Potteries. The Peak District provided the departure point from the Midlands and the beginning of the northern section, via the Pennines and the Yorkshire Dales. The route through Scotland swirled through the border country, before climbing towards Fort William and the glorious Highlands. It meandered along the west coast before taking a final swing to the north-east, across the sparse Sutherland moorland. The route concludes with a final flurry of bagpipe music, tartan and Irn-Bru at the finishing line in John o' Groats.

An open road is just a story waiting to be told. Find your own story on a Royal Enfield motorcycle today.

Well, that's how the marketing strapline goes, and it must have worked because I bought one. I bought my shiny new Classic 500 in March 2017. It looked like a restored original from the 1950s, and that's most people's first impression. The appearance of the bike has developed at geological pace since the 1950s and what you get now, from the factory in India, is a retro-looking bike with classic looks but with modern electronics and ABS disc-braking. It remains a simple machine, with a single-cylinder four-stroke engine that boasts, or rather timidly admits to, twenty-seven brake horsepower. That simplicity is also an endearing trait and a great positive, however. It means you can perform most mechanical repairs with an adjustable spanner, a big hammer and a roll of duct tape. It's an old-fashioned thumper of a motorbike. Aficionados will tell you that the distinctive vibration experienced if anyone is crazy enough to try speeds above fifty mph comes about because the piston remains still while the rest of the bike goes up and down. The only 'extras' added to the factory specifications of my motorcycle were a windscreen (for attaching tacky tourist stickers), a satnav mount and a custom-built rear rack courtesy of Bill, my engineer big brother. The rack was used to support twin (bicycle) pannier bags which, along with a small tank bag, carried all my belongings for the whole trip.

I understand from someone he met on the way that John Hillaby undertook his classic walk in 1966. Although the precise details aren't revealed, his journey was around 1,100 miles long, took three months to complete, and he set off in the second week of April. He doesn't say as much, but I assume two significant planning constraints dictated his timing. First, having to avoid the Scottish mid-summer midge season, and second, the need to be back for the 1966 World Cup finals in July. It was much the same for me, because 2018 was also a World Cup year. There were to be two significant cup final differences for me: being able to watch the finals in colour – and the outcome.

For his planning and preparations before his great walk, John Hillaby spent months reading and note-taking in the British Library. His preparations were thorough and an essential element of his successful writing formula. Nowadays we have it so easy – the world is available on our laptop screens through a simple search on the World Wide Web. I also tried to prepare for my trip thoroughly. I had the Internet to help with my research and a considerable library of maps and travel books. My story would develop as I journeyed through Great Britain, but before I left, I needed to plot my route as close as possible to that of John Hillaby's and to identify other places of interest to visit along the way. I did my homework, got my Royal Enfield serviced, charged my laptop and packed my bags. For the rest, to paraphrase the great man – I shall try to relate what I saw when I set off from Land's End in the fourth week of May 2018.

Another Journey through BRITAIN
Overview Map

1. Land's End to Mary Tavy
2. Mary Tavy to Minehead
3. Minehead to Taunton
4. Taunton to Hay-on-Wye
5. Hay-on-Wye to Oswestry
6. Oswestry to Wash
7. Wash to Elland
8. Elland to Malham
9. Malham to West Woodburn
10. West Woodburn to Callander
11. Callander to Beauly
12. Beauly to Gairloch
13. Gairloch to Lochinver
14. Lochinver to Bettyhill
15. Bettyhill to John o' Groats

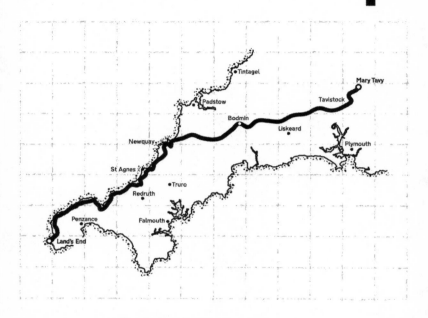

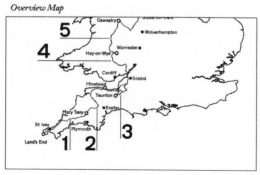

Overview Map

LAND'S END TO MARY TAVY

Day one of *Another Journey through Britain* began in Penzance Youth Hostel. I had no problem in getting up early and soon found myself sitting in the dining room, tucking into a hearty breakfast fry-up of eggs, bacon, beans and hash browns. It set me up for the day. In a rare display of successful multitasking, I was simultaneously tracing the route of the day's ride on the *Ordnance Survey Landranger Sheet 204*. As I visualised the journey and chose the stops along the way, I occasionally glanced over the top of the map to observe the other guests. Sitting on his own at the table in front of me, a crop-haired young lad, about 20 years old, shovelled down some porridge. His muscles burst out of an undersized T-shirt. He appeared to be a tattoo artist's demo model and was the nearest thing in that youth hostel to a youth. At sixty-three, I was probably the second youngest. That guy must have brought the average age of the breakfast group down to about sixty. I immediately had him down as a professional footballer – taking every spoonful of porridge as it comes. To be fair, he'd nearly finished his porridge but was looking for that extra bit of quality in the final third. I quickly admonished myself for such an unjustified and reactive bit of pigeonholing. In hindsight, I wish I'd just had a chat with him.

As I came to the end of my full English breakfast, with a satisfying finale of toast and marmalade, there was a burst of activity as more hostellers arrived, but still not enough to bring the average age in the room down to much below fifty-five.

The demographic mix on display that morning didn't surprise me. I recalled a conversation with the warden of the Elmscott Youth Hostel in north Devon two days earlier, while on my way down to Cornwall. He told me that us 'old 'uns' were keeping the hostels going. The 'Youth Hostel Association' (YHA) name is a bit of a misnomer. It's the older generation that has the time, the means and the interest to stay in hostels these days. We are keeping the organisation financially afloat. I'm simplifying the situation, but the general point is valid; it's the baby boomers, who began hostelling as youths, who appear to be the main users of the hostel network today. Sad in some ways, but in another way it's good to see so many silver-haired adventurers continuing their outdoor experiences into their sixties, seventies and beyond. More power to their anoraks, I say. I finished my cup of tea and got my things together to leave. I wanted to get down the road and get my adventure started. I paid up, got the bike loaded, fired her up and set off down the A30.

From the Penzance Youth Hostel to the car park at the Land's End visitor centre is a brief ride of about nine miles. The slightly overcast morning was forecast to turn into a beautiful day once the sun had burnt its way through the early mist and murk. In no time at all, I was at the starting point for my Land's End to John o' Groats adventure. Right, here we go!

The land ends – it does what it says on the tin, not that there's much of that once precious stuff left these days. Although tin mining was still just about a going concern back in the 1960s, when John Hillaby passed through Cornwall, the writing was already on the shaft wall by then, and the last tin mine fell silent in 1998.

The name Land's End derives from the Middle English name of Londeseynde, which can be traced back to 1337. The simple descriptive name seems to fit the bill pretty well... as far as England goes, this is the end of the land. Cornwall is the last county standing. Or the first, depending on your approach. The south-western tip of the mainland finally ends at this rocky promontory. A buttress of 200-foot-high grey granite stands guard at the door of the nation, with the swirling Atlantic Ocean at its feet. The cliffs maintain a brave act of defiance that has lasted for millennia as the irresistible force of the North Atlantic repeatedly attacks the immovable object of Cornwall. These cliffs are the dogged heavyweight, putting up a plucky fight over the years, fending off the blows of the lightweight sea with impressive stamina. The opponent is relentless though, repeatedly landing its punches, day and night. It's a geological war of attrition. The Cornish granite has been a worthy first line of defence. Anything less, perhaps a middleweight Portland limestone or a lightweight Devonian sandstone, would have thrown the towel in long ago... Land's End could have been in Devon by now.

I arrived at an empty visitors' car park just after 9 am. Everything lay ahead of me, my two weeks of adventure was about to begin, and it felt tingly exciting.

It's a new dawn, it's a new day, it's a new life for me, ooh... and I'm feeling good!

The jukebox selector in my head had, once again, automatically clicked into action, found the right song for the occasion, and played. No conscious input from me; it just happens.

I switched off the engine, dismounted the bike and rocked it back onto the stand. I took my crash helmet off and slowly filled my lungs with some North Atlantic ozone. I paused and looked beyond the car park out to sea. I moved in slow motion. That was partly because I'm in my sixties, but also to savour the moment. It was eerily silent and there was a quiet calm about the place; where was everyone?

I didn't want to hang around. Apart from the risk of attracting an unwanted parking charge, the tourist traps at either end of the Land's End to John o' Groats route aren't its most beautiful features. Well, I'll be honest, to me they're horrendous eyesores. I had mixed feelings about being there. It was super exciting to be starting my road trip, but I'm not so keen on the retail opportunities that the end to end terminals have become. I can't help feeling that things would be so much better if those nice people at the National Trust were in charge. As I wandered around the empty shops, the place seemed deserted, which I hadn't been expecting. Then I saw an opening time sign; things would get underway at 10 am.

I don't think I was missing much to be truthful, but somewhat hypocritically I had been hoping to buy that touristy Land's End sticker to go on my bike's windscreen.

One positive consequence of my early arrival was that the man who operates the iconic Land's End signpost was still in bed. There are special signposts at both ends of the journey. For a few pounds, the signpost owner will adjust the sign to show the distance to wherever you want: 'Oswestry 380 miles' for example. On this day, I had the signpost for free, as long as I didn't mind the sign showing the distance to New York instead of my hometown of Oswestry. Fortunately, the only other person up and about at that early hour arrived at that very moment with her pooch, Mixey. As we were the only ones there, we had a quick chat and exchanged favours, the lady taking my picture and me taking one of her and Mixey. The shops were not about to open, so I saddled up and headed out. I felt disappointed after all the anticipation of arriving for what should have been one of the big moments on my trip.

I rode about three miles up the road to the nearest habitation, the tiny and pretty hamlet of Sennen. I parked up in front of the impressive 13th-century church, which was also right next to the first and last pub in England. Although I wouldn't say I'm a religious person, the church lifted my spirits as I entered to check it out, which I suppose is what it's there to do – job done. Inside, it was a lovely tranquil place. There was a slightly musty and damp feeling and a calm atmosphere. It felt like someone had put a cold flannel on my forehead and said: 'There, just close your eyes... and relax'.

The structure and fittings of the church were like a museum. Precisely fashioned masonry and carpentry, built and maintained over centuries, displayed the caring devotion of the craftsmen (and possibly craftswomen) involved. Someone had lovingly created works of art in that place, rather than knocked out everyday objects to earn a living. Everything seemed perfectly proportioned and in its right place. It was all rather splendid and a soothing antidote to the retail vulgarity down the road. It cheered me up after my deflating Land's End experience.

Now I have to admit, I like a respectful look around a church graveyard when I visit somewhere and there's nothing wrong with that. It might seem a bit of a morbid fascination but amongst those sad epitaphs lie valuable clues to the social history of the area. I ventured from the calm protection of the church into the graveyard outside. The inscriptions on many of the gravestones painted a vivid picture of the precarious day-to-day existence of previous generations. There was a poignant memorial to the seafarers who perished on the nearby Brison rocks in 1851. You can find similar epitaphs in graveyards all around the south-west coastline.

By the time I'd finished looking around inside and outside the church, I had whiled away almost an hour, and as it was only a five-minute ride back to Land's End, I popped back to see if I could get that tacky sticker. The car park was filling up rapidly and it all looked very different to the place I'd left an hour earlier.

It was just gone 10 am, and one by one the shops and attractions sprang into life. I dashed in to get the sticker.

While I was there and because it wouldn't cost me anything, I had a quick look around the 'End to End' exhibition. I have to admit, despite my previous scepticism, it was rather good. The exhibition provided a fascinating insight into the weird and wonderful methods people have used over the years to make the iconic journey. They even had a Royal Enfield on display, which I took as a good omen.

As I emerged from the exhibition, the sight of the Shaun the Sheep and Arthur's Quest experiences opening up for another day brought me crashing back down to earth. An abandoned and rusting coke machine propped up against a wall seemed to sum up my view of the place – it held the promise of something cool and exciting but was essentially just empty. How depressing. It could all be so much better. But I was determined to stay positive. It was day one of my adventure. Land's End is still an extraordinary place, well worth a visit, and the name remains one of the most iconic in Britain. And anyway, who was I to talk, I'd just returned to buy a tacky sticker.

By the time I got back to the bike, things were hotting up. A steady stream of vehicles headed through the entrance and snaked its way into the main car park. Everyone else, except Mixey's owner and me it seemed, must have known that the place didn't get going until 10 am. I headed out of Land's End for a second time, this time to start my LeJog journey for real.

The plan for the day's ride was to head north along the coast road to Newquay. I'd then cut inland in a gentle curve to the western fringes of Dartmoor. It would be about 150 miles. The first part of the ride took me to the village of St Just to look at the Bronze Age chambered tomb at Carn Gluze, near to Cape Cornwall. I wonder how many place names in Cornwall begin with St? It must be the holiest county in Britain.

The chambered tomb of Ballowall Barrow at Carn Gluze is one of scores of prehistoric remains scattered over this most south-westerly part of England. The site of what is thought to be a large burial monument is gloriously positioned on the clifftops, looking out across the North Atlantic. It shows that the Bronze Age builders were keen to honour their ancestors with a splendid view. Modern-day estate agents would kill for such a grand-design location. I parked up and wandered around the ruins, trying my best to put myself in the sandals of someone from thousands of years ago.

I struggle to keep in perspective the thousands of years between the Ice Age and the Romans' arrival in Britain. It's hard to imagine the changes that were happening over such a lengthy period and the terminology can be confusing. So, I have my own very simplified version, which you can see below. In the next few paragraphs, I've laid out the dates, the periods and the changes taking place in Britain, as I understand them. There were no clear-cut change-over dates from one time period to the next. The edges are blurred, and changes would have been happening at different speeds in various parts of Britain, the rest of Europe and the world beyond. Sources will give differing versions of these dates, but if a simple summary helps – this is the timeline as I see it:

- Pre 10,000 BC (Stone Age Part 1 – Palaeolithic Period) Although there is some evidence to suggest that various species of humans occupied Britain several hundred thousand years ago, let's accept, for simplicity's sake, that there was nothing much happening before the Ice Age... about 10,000 BC.
- 10,000–6,000 BC (Stone Age Part 2 – Mesolithic Period) When the ice melted (some people suggest ten degrees warming over just a few decades), people from what is now central and eastern mainland Europe moved in and occupied Britain. At first, they would have been nomadic hunter-gatherers.
- 6,000–2,500 BC (Stone Age Part 3 – Neolithic Period) Domestication of animals and farming started by

about 4,000 BC and took about 2,000 years to spread across all parts of the British Isles. Having cracked agriculture, the inhabitants then organised themselves into social groups with static communities and tribal leaders.

- 2,500–800 BC (Bronze Age) and 800 BC–AD 43 (Iron Age) Britain gradually became more organised in terms of social groups and farming techniques. Some form of common language and currency developed. Iron Age man discovered that iron could improve farming productivity with the use of ploughs and other farming implements. Just as importantly, people had the means to produce lethal weaponry such as swords and axes. This was very handy for the turf wars that broke out as the population grew and tribal groups fought over the best bits of land. Britain's population had become weaponised. As well as providing equipment for farming the land, iron gave our ancestors the tools to fight for it.

- The Romans turned up in AD 43. We know what they did for us, and the rest is history.

I was fortunate to come across a party of tourists being shown around the Carn Gluze site by a local archaeologist. I tagged along in the background and listened to the discussion. It seems the mining rubble that covered the area for many years had helped to preserve it. I kept a respectful distance but remained in earshot and discretely took notes. The guide informed us that – and I paraphrase according to my rather sketchy note-taking – recent DNA evidence indicates that almost 12,000 years ago, as glaciers receded, nomadic hunter-gatherers migrated to the British Isles via a land bridge that extended from continental Europe. Excellent, that fitted my model as depicted above. According to the guide, the incomers were likely to have been dark-haired and dark-skinned people, who probably originated quite a way further south and east. Around 6,000 years ago, more migrants turned up from the Mediterranean area to follow those early adopters. The Beaker folk then arrived from Eurasia about 4,400 years ago and occupied the British mainland. Within a few generations, very few of the population of Britain were descendants of the former Neolithic farmers; nearly all of us were Beaker folk. I kept up with the group while frantically scribbling this stuff down and trying, but failing, to keep an image of Dr Bunsen Honeydew's assistant from the *Muppets* out of my head. The Beaker folk appeared in the late Neolithic period according to this local archaeologist. And he sounded like he knew his stuff. I was happy with this because it all accorded reasonably well with my simplified model.

When the tourist group moved up the footpath to study another site, I stopped to look around Carn Gluze a while longer and reflect on what I'd just heard. Mediterranean and Eurasian people? I thought about the Brexit vote a couple of years earlier, and all the comments made about wanting to ban freedom of movement, clamp down on immigration and return Britain to the British. What is British anyway? It just depends on what arbitrary point in time you choose to begin the argument. Brits are all post-Ice Age immigrants. If you go back around 2.5 million years, we're all East African.

This part of west Cornwall is just bursting with prehistoric sites. You almost fall over them everywhere you go. It's a treasure trove for archaeologists; there must be many remains still waiting to be discovered and properly examined. John Hillaby went to some length to describe the various monuments he came across on this same stretch of the Cornish coast, but he was unhappy with the way the archaeological sites were being managed – or not managed as he saw it. This is something that has improved over the years. Most of the sites are now well documented and the most significant ones have been designated as scheduled ancient monuments.

This means the sites belong to a group of over 20,000 in England that are considered nationally significant and protected by legislation. Carn Gluze, for example, is now under the guardianship of English Heritage, and managed by the National Trust. These protected sites now have detailed information boards for visitors. The one at Carn Gluze describes the monument, has a diagram showing a cross-section through the barrow and a photograph of William Copeland Borlase, who was responsible for the first official excavation in 1878. I'm sure John Hillaby would have approved of the extra care and attention the sites are now getting.

I swung my leg over the Royal Enfield again and rode up the coast a few miles further to Botallack – I was now in deepest Poldark country. I wanted to see the iconic and picturesque Crowns Engine Houses, two small 19th-century granite buildings that cling precariously to the cliff face, looking out to sea. The buildings used to contain winding gear and pumps to service the tin mines. A brief walk from the car park and I'd arrived. It was quite a scene. Steep granite cliffs, part grassed and bursting with spring wildflow-ers, plummeted down to the North Atlantic. The sun shone in all its glory and long blue rollers to the west queued up in parallel lines. As they arrived, they pounded the rocks, creating a foaming mass of white water that rumbled away at the base of the cliffs. The occasional spume of spray shot upwards to an appreciative roar of approval from the milky cauldron below.

Mining in Cornwall dates back to 1,000–2,000 BC when metal traders from the eastern Mediterranean turned up; an excellent early example of freedom of movement. I wonder if they would pass the 'skilled jobs' points criteria to get a visa in post-Brexit Britain. The visitors named Britain, the 'Cassi-terides' or 'Tin Islands'. They found tin fragments deposited in the gravel of stream beds. Some tin lodes emerged on the cliffs, where the metal could be easily gathered. The early miners followed the veins inland and from around the 16th century, they mined the tin underground. Looking at the deserted clifftops today, it's hard to imagine just how huge the tin and copper industry became back in its heyday, in the hundred years between 1750 and 1850. Cornwall was one of the most productive mining areas in the world and even as recently as the end of the 20th century Cornwall and Devon provided most of the UK's tin, copper and arsenic. At its peak, the tin and copper industries in these parts employed thousands of people. There were 600 steam engines and a labyrinth of underground tunnels stretching out over a mile under the Atlantic. By the end of the 19th century, more abundant and easily mined tin and copper deposits were discovered in places like Australia and South America. The extra supply brought about a crash in prices and it was the beginning of the end for Cornish tin mining. The last mine to close, South Crofty, hung on until 1998.

I felt guilty that my visit to such a spectacular UNESCO World Heritage Site was little more than a box-ticking exercise. I needed more time. The engine houses, clinging manfully to the cliffs, looked picturesque in the late spring sunshine, but they weren't such romantic places in their day. It's impossible to imagine the harsh lives of the poor miners, who had to stoop and work in the cold, damp and dark, with candles to light the way in the low shafts that went out under the sea. The Boscawen shaft, for example, went out for 2,500 feet under the Atlantic and the miners worked with pickaxes, perhaps only forty feet below the seabed. They could sometimes even hear the roar of the sea above them. It's no surprise that accidents and loss of life were frequent.

The sight before me at that moment was breath-taking – straight out of the tourist brochure. I stayed a while to take it all in, get some more photos and savour the moment. I'd mark it down for another visit, which was something that happened often on my trip.

Sometimes I'm asked why I go travelling and sometimes I

even ask myself. You know, the old clichés – what are you looking for? What can you find that's not already inside you? But when I am on my travels and experience something exceptional like the view at Botallack, I know why. I was only a few hours into day one of my adventure, but it was already 'one of those days'. You can read all the best travel guides and atlases, watch superb documentaries and browse the most fantastic Internet sites but it doesn't compare with the multi-sensory immersion of being somewhere like that on a day like that. Birds flying high. They knew how I felt. Botallack provided a sensory barrage: the salty smell of the Atlantic rollers and the sound as they boomed on the rocks below. The sight of the kittiwakes wheeling over the sea against a cobalt blue backdrop, catching the wind as it rose over the cliffs. I reminded myself – *this* is why I go travelling. Not everyone wants to and not everyone can. One day I might not be able to, so for the moment, I count myself lucky.

Friendly Lisa at the National Trust café at Botallack gave me some useful local knowledge for my next stopover. It enabled me to park fairly close to the megalithic monument of Chûn Quoit, just a few miles further to the east on Woon Gumpus Common. Where do they get those names? I only had to walk about a mile from the roadside parking spot Lisa had kindly directed me to, to visit the site.

Chûn Quoit is one of the many Neolithic structures scattered around the district of Penwith. It was another place visited by John Hillaby and another site with a magnificent view. There is a severe danger that visitors to west Cornwall may suffer ancient monument fatigue and move on to the next tourist stop without really appreciating just how magnificent each place is. I was guilty of that on such a whistle-stop tour through the countryside.

I don't think the beauty of the outlook from these monuments is entirely accidental. Those Neolithic forebears surely positioned them where they did for a reason. Whether that was to honour their dead with an excellent view to keep them entertained in their afterlives, to mark a route waypoint, or to make a statement to the local inhabitants, we'll never know.

Chûn Quoit – Neolithic chamber tomb

Chûn Quoit is a very distinctive monument that looks quite lonely on the open moorland. You can see it for miles around. It has four upright stones topped with a massive capstone at about head height, so it resembles a giant mushroom. These distinctive types of megalithic tomb are known as dolmens. Inside the mushroom there is a small and draughty chamber just about big enough for a human to squat in, for those sufficiently determined or stupid enough to try it.

John Hillaby had been determined enough to try it fifty years ago, but sensibly gave up because he was worried about getting stuck inside the ancient monument. I, on the other hand, was stupid enough to try it. It took a lot of effort; I had to breathe out to make myself small enough to wriggle into the space between two uprights, under the capstone. Inside the chamber it was eerily silent. There were some grasses and ferns laid out as though an offering, which made me feel like a guilty imposter. I squatted there like an idiot for a few minutes, realising I shouldn't be there. The silence continued but was interrupted by a whistle of wind between the upright rocks, prompting me to think about getting out again. For a moment, I speculated on how long it would take for anyone to find me, if I was stuck. What if no one questioned why someone had left a motorbike at the side of a lonely Cornish lane and thought it was just dumped there by joyriders? My LeJog adventure might have come to a premature end on day one. I didn't want to dwell on the subject. I was already feeling stupid enough, trapped inside a megalithic monument and not sure if I was offending the original occupants, so I breathed out, wriggled a lot and emerged sheepishly to resume my journey. While I don't expect for a minute that anyone would follow my adventure in the same way that I'm following John Hillaby's, I feel at this point I should add some words of wisdom gained from my experience: out of respect, and for your own safety, please don't attempt to squat in Chûn Quoit.

My route took me on to St Ives and then to Newquay, continuing loosely in the footsteps of John Hillaby. There was a lovely twisty road on the way into St Ives. It was a motorcyclist's delight. I was happily swaying one way and then the other gently around the bends, taking in the lovely Cornish lanes, breathing in the fresh air, in a world of my own. From nowhere, some maniac biker came screaming right up behind me like a bat out of hell... cue the Meatloaf backing track. I'm not sure if bats ride motorbikes, in hell or elsewhere, but you get my drift. This jerk flew past, God knows how fast and disappeared in a cloud of dust. It was like something out of the Isle of Man TT races. I was taken aback and seriously wondered if he'd make it to St Ives in one piece, riding like that. Bloody idiot! We clearly had different two-wheel objectives: I was on my leisurely road trip while he was on a white-knuckle adrenalin ride. I took a few deep breaths and settled back into my gentle morning ride.

St Ives was beautiful, as always. Without the tourists, it is a delightful, small, seaside resort with cobbled streets and picturesque fishermen's cottages. The town sits on a small peninsular jutting into the Atlantic. On one side of the headland is a sandy surfers' beach and on the more sheltered south-east side is a picture-postcard fishing harbour. When I arrived, however, the town was ridiculously busy with visitors, even that early in the season. I rode around the centre of town and down to the harbour, looking for somewhere to park. After two fruitless circuits, I settled for just stopping at the side of the road next to the harbour wall. I sat astride the bike for a few minutes, got a photo and admired the scene. There was a constant stream of pedestrians walking past me, all shapes and sizes, ages and backgrounds. Ice cream was a common theme, and I felt the urge for a double honeycomb and vanilla. Just then a young lad, probably in his late teens, rushed enthusiastically up to me with the broadest of smiles on his face. He shook my hand vigorously and introduced himself. Like the guy in Penzance Youth Hostel, this chap was seriously over-tattooed. There wasn't much spare skin left to decorate. I didn't have time to make rash pigeonhole judgements this time.

'You must be the guy I just passed on the way into town on the twisty', he said. 'I recognise the old Royal Enfield: what a beauty!'

Ah, the superbike speedster who passed me at warp speed earlier. He turned out to be from the village of Mullion. The fella couldn't have been more friendly and charming. We exchanged stories about our bikes, his being a bored-out 175cc something or other that I probably shouldn't describe further for risk of incriminating the poor guy. OK, so it wasn't a superbike, but I bet he could do the Zennor run in less than twelve parsecs. He told me how he knew that twisty like the back of his hand and loved to lay the bike over until he could feel the hedgerows brushing his shoulders.

'Oh yeah, same here mate', I said, 'you can't beat it'.

We parted with high fives, the best of biker buddies.

I remembered that St Ives was where John Hillaby had met a fisherman who was outraged at seeing a beatnik bathing naked at dusk. It's hard to imagine such indignation now. I looked hard, for research purposes, but there weren't any naked girls on this occasion. There was more of a middle-aged than youthful feel to the place. I guess all the rebellious teenagers go to Ibiza these days and get naked there.

The local constabulary had run John Hillaby out of town for sleeping rough back in 1966. He was told he was contravening the Vagrancy Act. That's something that has changed for the worse over the last fifty years, despite the increased standard of living. I remember as a kid seeing the odd tramp walking along the road, but not the numbers of rough sleepers you now see in all the major towns and cities... what happened?

Maybe when I was younger I didn't notice that sort of thing, but statistics suggest that the situation has gradually deteriorated. The Vagrancy Act of 1824 is still in force in England and Wales and hundreds of prosecutions take place every year. For 2018, the government estimated the number of people sleeping rough in the UK was just over 4,500. This figure had doubled since 2010 with poverty and lack of housing cited as two of the more obvious contributory factors. Around 88 per cent of these people are men. Does this mean that women are less likely to become homeless or do they have ways of dealing with it that doesn't result in them being out on the street? Are they prevented from leaving home, physically or emotionally? I'm sure it's not a simple issue but the homeless statistics are not a great reflection on our so-called social and economic progress.

Newquay didn't seem to have improved much since my wife and I lived in Cornwall in the 1980s. Sorry, Newquay, it's just a personal view. The beaches are still amazing, but the town isn't so pretty with wall to wall surf shops, surf hostels, fast-food outlets and pubs – and more surf shops. It was cool when I was a teenager – but now, as an oldie, I couldn't get out of town fast enough.

I rode out to St Mawgan where, back in 1966, John Hillaby had taken a shortcut across the military airfield and stumbled into some gipsies grazing their horses. Official noticeboards warned him to keep out of the area and funnily enough, those noticeboards are still there. RAF St Mawgan has now become Cornwall Airport Newquay. Noticeboards warn potential intruders about RAF police dogs on patrol and let you know that the airfield is a prohibited place under the Official Secrets Act. No problem there, I thought; I signed up as a civil servant in the 1970s. I went in for a cup of tea before riding on towards Camborne and Redruth.

I was enjoying perfect conditions for motorcycle riding and I loved the gentle roar and rhythmic thump of the bike engine as I cruised through Cornwall. The town names got me thinking back to over thirty years earlier, when my wife and I moved to Cornwall. They were joyful days, as we began family life with our first son, Tom. I was an Ordnance Survey (OS) surveyor based in Truro. From there, our team of four surveyors kept the maps of the county up to date. Riding today in the footsteps of John Hillaby, and revisiting places that had been in 'my patch' all those years ago, got the nostalgia juices flowing. My boss, Keith Kingdom, was an inspiration to a relatively young surveyor still fumbling on the lower rungs of a somewhat wobbly career ladder. To be honest, my career wasn't my top priority in those days. What left a lifelong impression on me though was Keith's positive and optimistic attitude to everything; nothing was impossible, it was all doable… and let's bloody well enjoy it along the way! The phrase that sticks in my memory is the one he always used on those many bright Cornish mornings when he'd burst into the office at around 8 am to announce in his rustic West Country accent, 'It's a great-to-be-alive day!' He was right. They were great-to-be-alive days. And so was day one of my road trip as I continued to make my way inland.

I stopped off to look at the old tin mine at South Crofty. Although the last mine closed over 20 years ago, there are potentially exciting times ahead for Cornwall. New technologies such as robotics, electric vehicles and power storage have caused a big rise in demand for lithium, which is a light metal, often found alongside tin. The rocks under Cornwall might soon become very significant once again. There are reports of plans to pump out the millions of cubic metres of water that have flooded South Crofty. Depending on what they find, and the economics of removal, it might be possible to start the extraction of lithium there, and elsewhere in Cornwall.

Wheal Coates – former tin mine

From South Crofty I headed back up to the north coast to find Wheal Coates ('wheal' is Cornish for mine). It's another very recognisable former mining site that looks out into the Atlantic from high on the clifftops. In a tick-box dash through Cornwall, this was another of my 'must-do' stop-off locations. In 2006, they gave the old mine UNESCO World Heritage Site status, which puts it on a par with the Taj Mahal, the Great Wall of China and the Pyramids. You wouldn't want to miss this one.

By now, the sun was blazing, and it was like a proper summer's day. To help find the best spot to view the former mine buildings at Wheal Coates I stopped off at the museum at St Agnes and was so glad that I did. It was a little treasure trove and the person on duty that day was extremely friendly and helpful. I carried on to Wheal Coates. The National Trust car park sits in a deep cleft in the cliffs and was being looked after by two most delightful young ladies. Not only did they refuse payment for parking for an hour (I made that up if anyone might get into trouble) but they also volunteered to look after my panniers and crash helmet, so I wouldn't have to cart them with me on the walk to and from the mine workings.

The trail is relatively short and well worth the effort as you can't see the main attractions from the car park. When you come around the corner of the clifftop walk and first catch sight of the Towanroath Pumping Engine House, you immediately recognise one of the most iconic images of Cornwall. One that has graced many a calendar, book cover and tourist poster. The little pump house and chimney sits proudly on the clifftop with a vast expanse of blue sea as a backdrop. I sat there in the sun, on the tufted cliff grass admiring the view, every bit the spoilt tourist. As I tucked into the Cornish pasty that I'd taken with me, the old tin miners' staple food, I tried to imagine the harsh reality of life for those 19th-century workers.

Travelling around Cornwall it's impossible not to notice the impact made by wind farms. The current scene would have been hard to imagine in John Hillaby's time. Back in 1966, we were dabbling with our first attempts at nuclear power in the UK, and it wasn't until the 1980s and 1990s that renewable energy came into play seriously. The first commercial installation in Cornwall was the Delabole wind farm in

1991, comprising four turbines. As I write, there are over 500 wind turbines in Cornwall and over 10,000 in the UK as a whole. Those in Cornwall generate around 141 MW of energy and over the whole of the country the contribution made by onshore wind power is almost 10 per cent of our total needs or enough to power over seven million homes. Even more productive in terms of energy creation are solar farms, which are another relatively recent arrival. There are almost 3,000 acres of Cornwall covered by solar farms, and they generate an impressive 500 MW of energy. In a neat juxtaposition of old and new, the 7.2 acre Wheal Jane solar farm, near Truro, was the biggest of its kind in Britain when it was switched on in 2011. It sits atop the former tin mine of the same name and contributes 1.4 MW of electricity, which is enough for around 430 homes. Onshore renewables are a bit of a Marmite issue. Most people can put up with the change of view in exchange for the clean fuel benefits – unless perhaps it's your view in your backyard.

Riding into Bodmin brought back memories of my first jury service back in the 1980s. The trial I attended was one of the last in the old county courtroom in Bodmin. In that musty old wood-panelled courtroom, it wasn't difficult to conjure up images of pirates and wreckers from years gone by. My case was a somewhat less romantic, but no less sad, story of shoplifting.

I rode on towards Tavistock, hoping to look in at the Copper Penny Inn at the strangely named hamlet of Chipshop: somewhere else visited by John Hillaby. I somehow rode straight past the junction though and missed the road to Chipshop. Let us call it a tactical change of route. Anyway, on a trip like this, my journey was flexible, and I was happy to go wherever the whim, or in this case, carelessness, took me. Sometimes random and unexpected paths can be better anyway. As HV Morton describes in the first page of the introduction to his book, *In Search of England,* (first published in 1927) some roads he followed 'led him aright, and some astray... the first were the most useful; the others were the most interesting'.

Having cruised unwittingly past the turning to Chipshop, I headed to Minions, a village on the eastern flank of Bodmin Moor. I was keen to visit the Hurlers, a group of early Bronze Age standing stones described by John Hillaby. There are three ancient circles there, thick with ceremonial remains and stones. The site and the village didn't disappoint. Local legend says the stones are the remains of men who became petrified after playing the game of hurling on the Sabbath. I'm more inclined to the theory that the three circles and the surrounding stones were pagan ceremonial sites and that early missionaries put the petrified sportsmen story out there to spook the locals, so they'd become God-fearing Christians. As my visit was on a Sunday, to be on the safe side, I had my fingers crossed in case motorcycle riding came under the same general sports category as hurling, or once again my road trip would come to a grinding halt on day one.

At this point, I remembered my intended Chipshop stopover – 'ah, bother!'... was close to what I really thought. Because I was getting near to my overnight stop, I decided I'd pop back to Chipshop in the morning. This flexibility was a luxury I had with a motorbike that John Hillaby couldn't possibly have enjoyed while walking. I don't imagine he would have wanted to return even six or seven miles if he could help it, with another 1,000 miles still to go. I continued on to my lodgings for the night, the 16th-century Elephant's Nest pub near Mary Tavy on the western edge of Dartmoor. It was almost 150 miles from my journey's start at Land's End.

When John Hillaby visited the pub in 1966, he found the place full of local youths. He comments on the excruciatingly loud jukebox and seeing one girl who looked no more than fourteen. The young lads of Devon were dancing to the sound of 'I Wanna Hold Your Hand' by the Beatles. The description evokes a nostalgic image of the past, especially for a boy like myself, born in the 1950s. I even imagined the scene in black and white when I first read about it. Like the image of the naked beatnik in St Ives, it's a snapshot of a bygone age.

Although some pubs are still used by teenagers, many hostelries, like the Elephant's Nest, are now more often frequented by the older generation – those who might have been teens in the 1960s. Again, it's probably us old ones who have the time and means to do it. Pubs find it hard to survive these days, with four pubs going out of business every day in Britain. Business rates, big brewing conglomerates, cheap supermarket booze, declining disposable incomes and the smoking ban are all contributory reasons. The pubs that survive are the ones that adapt; they find ways of changing with the times. It's evolution. Some become sports bars, some turn to craft ales and some become micro-breweries, offering something different, perhaps with bars overlooking the brewing operation, for example. Developing the food offer is a clever strategy as there are higher margins on food and the changing social dynamic of pubs means that couples, families and oldies like me are the most likely visitors. Pubs are no longer just used by men as alehouses, as might have been the case a few decades ago.

The Elephant's Nest has gone down the restaurant route and also developed its overnight accommodation offer with some lovely luxury rooms. To broaden its appeal, it holds regular bingo and quiz nights. After a hectic day on the road, I felt more like a quiet night. I found my room, took a quick shower, and headed for the bar.

I found myself seated amongst a table of policemen and policewomen from the Staffordshire Constabulary, as you do, and a lively group from the local Young Farmers' Club. Now there's an interesting combination. Sometimes it's best not to think about it – just go with the flow. I had a brief chat with the law enforcers and got sucked into a sorry tale of urban degeneration in the Potteries.

'Oh, it's all charity shops, pound shops and out of town malls; where has the town centre gone?' asked a distraught

Woman Police Constable staring forlornly at the last mouthful of pinot grigio in the bottom of her glass. With that degree of urban decline in northern Staffordshire, perhaps she should have bought a large one. Well, it was an excellent question, and fortunately, it was a rhetorical one. I didn't have a ready answer, but the sad state of Britain's town centres was something I would see at first hand several times on *Another Journey through Britain*. For the time being, some sticky toffee pudding and an Irish coffee were easing the pain.

Before I departed to my room for the night, I asked around for an answer to the obvious question. The name of the inn is believed to be derived from a former owner who, let's say, was on the portly side. He spent his time behind the bar, perched on a stool. Someone told him he looked like an elephant on its nest (obviously, because that makes sense), and somehow the name stuck.

I drained my pint and thought back to the sights and incidents of the day. I was so lucky to have experienced a first day like that. Or any day like that. For most of the ride, I'd taken to the back roads; I'd hardly seen anything more than a B-road all day. One of the features of the day that stuck in my mind, and something I hadn't expected, was the number of wildflowers that lined the way along the Cornish lanes – amazing. If there had only been a hundred-metre stretch of them, people would travel for miles to see the sight. But there must have been hundreds of miles of them, and they were gorgeous. My thoughts turned to the next day's ride and whether it could match that first day. I checked the map to remind myself of the route and looked forward to my journey into Devon and up into Somerset.

Map **2**

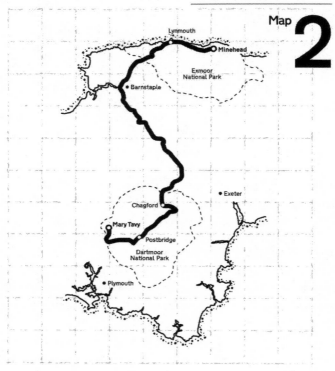

Overview Map

MARY TAVY TO MINEHEAD

What a delightful place to spend the night. I would describe the Elephant's Nest as off the beaten track, but its rural seclusion is one of the best things about it. A chap can find some peace in a place like that.

The unexpected sound of someone in the lane outside my bedroom window, clicking two coconut shells together, shattered the rural silence at 7 am on day two of my journey. I thought little more of it; there's not much else to do in those remote rural parts of the West Country. It's probably one of those quaint traditions that we should encourage before they die out.

I wandered down for breakfast and braced myself for what looked like a formidable full English. I wasn't going to mention the racket in the lane, but the landlord asked if I'd had a good night's sleep. He suggested that what I'd heard was his son setting off for work on his horse. What? Who does that in the 21st century? I'm sorry, but I know which version I think is more plausible.

A full English breakfast is a guilty pleasure when staying in a B&B, in this case, a 16th-century inn. And why not? It's not something I'd do at home, though. I didn't even have the excuse of needing the calories for a hard day's cycling.

Anyway, by the end I was stuffed. It was lovely, and it kept me going all day.

After my tactical route-amendment decision the previous evening, I was keen to get back to the hamlet of Chipshop first thing. I double-checked its location on the map before I left. I packed my bags and fired up the motorbike for another day of adventure. The weather forecast looked promising. A dry day is always the first thing I look for on the forecast whenever I go on a trip like this. After that, a sunny day is a bonus, and then a warm and not too windy day, please. It looked like I would get all of that on day two, and the next day as well. Fantastic!

I successfully navigated the tiny Devon lanes away from the Elephant's Nest and was soon back down the road, the right one obviously, in the aforementioned hamlet just outside Tavistock. I'm not sure what constitutes a hamlet, but if it's an inn and one or two other houses next to a road, then Chipshop is one. It wasn't even large enough to qualify for what my mother-in-law would call 'a one-eyed horse town'. John Hillaby had stayed in the Hare and Hounds back in 1966, but it looked like the establishment had been renamed the Copper Penny Inn.

Contrary to what you might think, the amusingly named village isn't named after the iconic gourmet food outlet. It dates from the 1800s when they paid the local copper and tin miners with tokens or 'chips'. Although the chips weren't legal tender, the miners could exchange them for food and drink in the local pub, which was the Chipshop Inn. The hamlet then got its name from the pub. Those hungry and thirsty miners would have been employed at the nearby Devon Great Consols, which was about a mile from the hamlet. I'm ashamed to say that I'd never heard of the place before my ride but get this – it was the site of what was once the most productive copper mine in the world. The site employed over 1,200 people at its peak back in the mid-19th century.

Demand for the metal was so high the copper couldn't be shifted out fast enough. The mine owners constructed a narrow-gauge railway to Morwellham Quay on the River Tamar, about four miles to the south, to ship copper and arsenic out to the rest of the world. The quay and mining area were yet another UNESCO World Heritage Site on my route. I felt guilty, once again, finding myself pushed for time and marking the place down as a must for a future visit.

John Hillaby described a boisterous night at the Hare and Hounds in Chipshop. He wrote that the bar shook with the sound of hymn singing, which he thought was mainly a result of the local cider. When I was there, there wasn't a sign of life, although it was first thing on a Monday morning. The inn looked like it was mainly used as a restaurant. As another hostelry looking for a way to survive, it had diversified. Notices advertised a skittles alley and a farm shop. It seemed they had regular functions – but no mention of hymn singing. I took a quick photo, popped back to Tavistock to top up with fuel, and headed eastwards towards Dartmoor.

My route continued on minor roads. John Hillaby had squelched cross-country from the Elephant's Nest to Cranmere Pool and onto the village of Postbridge, in the heart of Dartmoor. From there he headed north-east over more squelchy bogs to Chagford, on the eastern edge of the moor. I decided against a visit to the notorious bog at Cranmere Pool, which was just as well, as there is no road to it. Instead, I took two delightful B-roads right across the middle of the Dartmoor National Park to Postbridge, and then on to Chagford.

The centre of the National Park looked desolate even on a warm spring day, and it wasn't hard to imagine the place becoming foreboding in the middle of winter. I parked up on a wild and windswept open stretch of the moor near to a place called Two Bridges. I walked up the sparsely covered hillside for half a mile or so, following what must have been a sheep path, to the top of a tor – an outcrop of rounded granite for which Dartmoor is famous. Although it wasn't high, there was a glorious view of the rugged moorland into the distance with miles of tufted grass and peat bog interrupted by patches of bare earth and rock. The landscape was undulating and atop most hills there were scars of exposed granite and tors that looked like a giant had put together some outdoor rock sculptures. Although I had the place to myself, I was keen to get back to the bike. I didn't want some scallies coming along and liberating my panniers before I had the chance to sprint back down the hill. I scurried back to the bike after a momentary standoff on the path with another common sight in the area – half a dozen Dartmoor ponies. I was ticking all the Dartmoor tourist boxes.

The jukebox selector in my head once again came up with the right song for the moment. I joined in the backing vocals, belting them out full blast as I cruised north-eastwards along the B3212. It was my own 'Ventura Highway' in the sunshine that morning. I could sing like no one was listening because there was no one listening. The ride was turning into a great one again. I was so lucky. After yesterday, I didn't think I could get another day so good.

As I rode on towards Postbridge, bang in the centre of Dartmoor, I noticed the mileage on the odometer. As an aside, I've always thought 'odometer' was a strange word. Maybe it's the 'odd' bit at the beginning. An odometer sounds like an instrument you should use for measuring strangeness. Anyway, the odometer mileage was ticking over to 1981 – that's strange, the year I married my wife, Jan. I wouldn't usually take notice of the mileage, but perhaps I caught the numbers in my peripheral vision, and a message went to brain central to say: 'Hold up, something relevant is happening here, mate! Start the wedding memory synapse connection sequence'.

Shortly after that, in fact I can say with some certainty, five miles later, the mileage reached 1986, the year our oldest son, Tom, was born. By the time I'd reached Chagford, on the far side of the moor, our other two children, Sarah and Greg, had been born, grown up, been to university and all left home. The sad thing is that all those things seem to have happened just as quickly in real-time. I reflected on this in a mood of downwardly spiralling melancholy for a few minutes. Before I reached the Morrissey album and bottle of whisky stage, I gave myself a good talking to, and reminded myself how lucky I've been, and still am.

Onwards and upwards. I was counting my blessings with the weather as well. My ride progressed serenely, with hardly any other traffic around, to the centre of the National Park and the village of Postbridge. John Hillaby hadn't been nearly so lucky. He describes dense mist, rain, and ill-tempered route-finding across watery bogs during this section of the journey. Dartmoor comes across in Hillaby's book as hard-going and slightly depressing, and you get the impression that he was quite relieved to arrive at Chagford.

Postbridge is a charming place with an excellent visitor centre and a much-photographed 13th-century clapper bridge. The name is thought to derive from the Anglo-Saxon 'cleaca' which means 'bridge over the steppingstones'. Once again, it's hard to argue with that. The picturesque clapper bridge, just off the B-road, elegantly connects the two banks of the East Dart River. The construction of the bridge hadn't stretched the designer's imagination too much; large flat horizontal slabs of granite were laid on top of substantial vertical stone piers. This is minimalist functionality, but the result is beautiful in its proportions and position. 'Post' is the old Dartmoor name for the slabs, which explains the origin of the village name.

The mining background of the area was once again there to see. The bridge was originally used to carry packhorses taking tin to the stannary town of Tavistock. 'Stannary' isn't a word you're likely to use on a day-to-day basis – you might only come across it in Scrabble these days (11 points). It relates to tin mining, or in the case of a stannary town, such as Tavistock or Chagford, to somewhere they used to assess and sell the tin. John Hillaby described how in the 16th century, tinners became a powerful trade union, able to make their own laws and dish out their own punishment in stannary courts.

I resolved to take my time looking around the Postbridge visitor centre. I didn't want this to be yet another stopover where I just grabbed a quick photo and then mindlessly motored on to the next tourist highlight. I parked right outside the visitor centre entrance, where the motorbike could remain in sight most of the time, so I could leave the panniers on. The friendly staff were happy for me to leave my crash helmet and riding jacket behind the counter. While I'd been dismounting and removing my crash helmet, a party of German tourists appeared from a coach on the far side of the car park. They seemed to be most impressed with the Royal Enfield as they filed past and into the visitor centre. There wasn't much English spoken, but there were plenty of thumbs-up, smiles and knowing nods. They probably thought they were looking at a painstakingly maintained original from the 1950s. Well, yes, but that was just me. I felt quite pleased with myself, smiling appreciatively and nodding back. I didn't have the heart, or the slightest knowl-edge of German, to tell them my Classic 500 was just over a year old and built in India.

By the time I emerged from the visitor centre, the day was warming up, so I popped into the village shop for a cold drink and some Devon fudge. Why not live the dream; I didn't know when I might be this way again. I slowly saun-tered down the road, in the warmth of the midday sun, towards the clapper bridge. It was a 'slow saunter' kind of day. Seeing some German tourists again, I even managed a bit of a swagger to go with my slow saunter, if you can swagger while sauntering without looking like Quasimodo. It wasn't far to the bridge, which looked quintessentially Dartmoor Park, and a veritable tourist magnet. There are other clapper bridges in the area apparently, some allegedly even more picturesque. This one is handily placed near to the road and the visitor car park, however, so it's the one everyone knows about, can reach easily and wants to visit. I left the road and walked up and down the banks of the East Dart, eying up the view of the bridge and looking for the killer photo spot. Every time I looked up at the clapper bridge ready to take a photo, it was covered in German tourists.

Clapper Bridge, Dartmoor

I waited. Patiently at first, then impatiently, and then even more impatiently. I just wanted a nice unpopulated photo. Every time a few of the group left, they were instantly replaced by others. At first, this was amusing – haha what a coincidence. But after a while, the novelty wore off. After what seemed like hours, but in reality, must have been about five minutes, I was staring up at the Germans with an exasperated expression and intense frustration. Eventually recognising me as the friendly but now red-faced motorcyclist they'd met back at the visitor centre, they greeted me like an old friend – all waves, with lairy shouting and stupid poses for my photo. Fantastic, guys! I'm stubborn though, and hours later (probably about 20 minutes), the place was at last empty. It had been a tactical triumph of attrition on my part; I knew the Germans would have to leave the bridge eventually or miss their coach. I got some half-decent photos and headed back to the bike. Onto Chagford then, across more miles of open moorland. Yet again, I was thinking: 'This is amazing, I must come back here one day soon'.

The market town of Chagford, near the River Teign, nestles on the eastern side of Dartmoor. I've seen it described as 'the jewel of Dartmoor'. John Hillaby found a cheery little town with a few pubs around a small market square. That's about right, I thought. As I rode into Chagford, I immediately liked it. It seemed a refined town, with an impressive church, a cricket ground, nice looking pubs, hotels and tearooms. The pubs were the sort that have wood panelling, courtyards and tasteful paintings rather than pool tables, loud music and live football. In the attractive town centre, you can find a bakery, a florist and an art gallery. Chagford wasn't a down at heel place like so many rural towns these days, full of nail bars, vape outlets and betting shops. Whatever formula they were using there, it was working. I liked it a lot, and by the end of *Another Journey through Britain*, this was the place I looked back on as my favourite town visited. I could happily live in Chagford. Parked in the road next to the church, I felt compelled to pop into the town's graveyard and inspect the stones. There was nothing much out of the ordinary, as far as I could tell with a cursory glance. I noticed an epitaph dedicated to an elderly gentleman who 'fell asleep on 23rd December 1888'. It made me think – 'Yes, Chagford is that kind of place'. Previous generations of Sennen's population had been dashed upon the rocks, but in tranquil Chagford, they gently fell asleep.

Back at the bike, a man approached me wanting to know all about it. That happened a lot on the trip; the bike seems to get the nostalgia juices flowing for men of a certain age. This chap had lived most of his life in Redditch, West Midlands, the traditional home of Royal Enfield with its original factory sited there in 1901. The factory closed in 1967, with production eventually moving out to India, and this fella had many happy memories of the factory and its influence on the town.

I rode on northwards to Yeoford. I was wondering if the Station Hotel, described by John Hillaby, was still there. It was, but now it was the Mare and Foal pub. The railway station was also still there, now part of a community railway line running from Exeter to Barnstaple. With the pub shut, and not much other sign of life, I motored on via tiny Devon lanes, to enjoy a quick burst on the A377, north to Barnstaple. That bit of road was a dream of a ride on a motorbike. In the early stages of the engine's life, the Royal Enfield 500 seems to have a sweet spot at around 40 mph (stop it bikers, please don't laugh). By the time you get to 50 mph, the vibrations become a bit much, which is a useful safety feature – a speed limiter that's hard to ignore. Up to 35 mph it's still gurgling nicely, but at 40 mph, everything seems to go into synch, calms down, and it's nice and smooth. I should add that a year after the ride, the engine was nicely worn in and the sweet spot had moved up to a more banter-friendly 50 mph. For those 20 miles up to Barnstaple, I had the road entirely to myself. Nothing caught up with me, and I didn't catch up with anyone. You wouldn't, would you, at that speed? For 20 miles, I was just leaning from left to right in a pleasant rhythm as the road swung one way then the next. Beautiful; it just felt right.

After Barnstaple, which brought back happy memories of my posting there with OS back in the 1980s, I headed eastwards over Exmoor, my second National Park of the day. Between Yeoford and Bridgwater, I was going somewhat off-piste. My logic was thus – I was not following John Hillaby's path exactly anyway because he walked, and I was on a motorbike. Our routes, therefore, couldn't be precisely the same. Secondly, the road up to Barnstaple, across the top of Exmoor and along the north Devon/Somerset coast was too beautiful to miss. So, I'd do my own thing and then join back with the original route somewhere around the Quantocks, just short of Bridgwater. I'm sure no one would mind.

The forty or so miles of the A39 from Barnstaple to Minehead is one of those must-do biker routes and one that I've seen described as the best road in the South West. It's another one that's full of gentle twists one way and then the other, with the odd hairpin and a few very steep hills thrown in, set amidst some stunning Exmoor scenery. It should be savoured rather than blasted through, but that's just me. The Mullion Missile might see it differently. I can imagine it could be a right pain if you got stuck behind a line of caravans, but on the right day and with an open road, that stretch takes some beating.

I was enjoying the ride almost too much, and it was all going too quickly. I dropped into Lynmouth to cool off for a while and take in the sunshine and the scenery. This pretty little coastal village lies at the end of a short gorge that contains the East and West Lyn Rivers, and links back to the village of Lynton, 600 feet higher up inland. Lynmouth is one of many coastal resorts that boomed in the Victorian times when the area around Lynton became known as Little Switzerland. A cute little water-powered funicular railway plods up and down between the villages of Lynmouth and Lynton. Sadly, Lynmouth is remembered for the terrible flooding that occurred in 1952. Nine inches of rain fell in 24 hours on 15th August that year. It funnelled through the gorge into a surging torrent that destroyed more than a hundred buildings and took thirty-four lives. Those tragic scenes were hard to imagine on the calm sunny day when I was there.

The weather was beautiful, and the tourist crowds were out in force. The place reminded me a bit of St Ives – hard to park and almost too many people to be comfortable. The air was seaside salty and the sun glistened on the water. Seagulls, grown fat on tourists' chips, serenaded a constant stream of visitors who were jostling their way up and down the pavement leading to and from the harbour. I was lucky to find a place to park next to another couple of touring bikes alongside the West Lyn River, on the accurately named Riverside Road. A seemingly endless row of cafés and pubs were scarcely keeping up with visitor demand for cool drinks and ice cream. I spotted a spare table right opposite where I'd parked and quickly dived over to grab it while I could. I asked for a cold drink and an ice cream and surveyed the surrounding scene. It was just the place for some people-watching. Maybe to differentiate itself from all the other cafés along this stretch of road, the one to which fate had delivered me had a unique refreshment on offer. Well, unique in my experience until then, and it was proving to be popular. A constant stream of caring dog owners popped in to treat their four-legged friends to doggy ice creams! And hang on, by quite a long way that's not the best bit.

On the table right next to me were Dave and Karen from Smethwick, Birmingham. My first thought was that their matching Aston Villa football jerseys were inappropriate for this genteel-looking former Victorian resort. But then again, apart from match day at Villa Park, where would those jerseys be appropriate? With them, precariously propped up in a child's highchair, was Vincent, their one-eared French bulldog, resplendent with a table napkin around his neck, being fed a double pistachio ice cream in a fancy cone by Karen. I know, it's barking… almost unbelievable. You had to be there. Poor dog, not having a full complement of ears wasn't his only issue; I swear he was squint-eyed and looking at both owner Karen and me at the same time. It was surreal, whichever way you look at it and definitely the way he looked at it. To his credit, Vincent was licking the ice cream properly, not trying to woof it all down in one go, as some other doggy visitors were. Those bits of Vincent not covered by a napkin or pistachio ice cream were a lovely light-brown Jersey cow colour and he had a stylish white stripe down the centre of his head. He was hard to ignore and was causing quite a stir. From where I was sitting, I could watch people walking down the pavement and see their reactions as they came to the café and spotted Vincent. Lynmouth appears to attract quite a lot of Midlanders, or it did on the day I was there. I think my favourite reaction was the middle-aged guy, with his two mates, who pronounced in a booming Brummie accent 'oh chuffin' hell, look at the bloody state of that!' I felt slightly embarrassed on Vincent's owners' behalf, but fortunately, Vincent couldn't give a toss.

I got chatting to Dave and Karen and learnt about their dog's background and his taste in ice cream. The special doggy ice cream at this café was perfect. They'd been in a few times and Vincent was gradually working his way through the menu with no adverse effects. They'd tried other ice creams in other establishments in the past but with mixed results. Standard ice cream is not always good for a dog's sensitive tummy. Vanilla was OK, but mint and choc chip from other cafés had made Vincent sick and tutti-frutti could result in a runny poo. Not a pleasant image and way too much information, I thought, as I worked my way through a vanilla and tutti-frutti double scoop. I didn't want to ask about the ear, but I was told about it, anyway. It resulted from a fight with another dog when Vincent was a puppy, before the current owners got him from a rescue home. They named him after the artist, obviously. Detecting a sense of humour in the choice of name, I was within a dog's whisker of saying 'Well, he's no oil painting'. I thought better of it, opting instead for, 'Oh no, the poor sausage' while looking suitably sympathetic. Hoping to lighten the mood by shifting the conversation to a common place of empathy and understanding, I added: 'The other dog must have been a Baggies fan'.

I'm not sure whether the owners' totally blank responses were from failure to grasp my clumsy attempt at humour or because they got it but didn't find it at all amusing. Perhaps the pain of the memory was all too much. Dave and I switched to the subject of deadly coastal floods while Karen helped Vincent to finish the last remains of the cone.

I left the doggy ice cream paradise that is Lynmouth and had a most enjoyable ride over Exmoor. It looked just like Dartmoor in the morning, but without the distinctive tors. On his route out of the West Country, John Hillaby skirted around the edges of Exmoor, so he only saw it from afar. His view on both National Parks was straightforward; he considered they were being slowly destroyed. To him, the problems with Dartmoor were to do with military exercises, overstocking and too much coniferous planting. He didn't like the development of reservoirs either, which continued to be constructed even after the establishment of the National Park in 1951. At the time of his *Journey through Britain*, there were ten National Parks in existence. Five more have been added in the 50 years since then, three in England and two in Scotland. On my trip, I would pass through seven of them.

Besides the National Parks, there are thirty-four Areas of Outstanding Natural Beauty (AONB) in England and Wales, less than half of which were in existence back in 1966. Being British, we have to make things complicated. In Scotland, they have two National Parks, forty-five National Nature Reserves, three UNESCO GeoParks and two UNESCO Biospheres. The original purpose of the Parks was to conserve and preserve, but also to open the areas up for visitors to enjoy. Nowadays, the National Parks cover approximately 10 per cent of England, 20 per cent of Wales and 7 per cent of Scotland. I see them as a significant success story, although it might depend on who you ask. The objectives of the National Parks and AONBs have to satisfy the needs of people living outside and inside those areas. Opening them up for walking, climbing, water sports, etc., has seen ever-increasing numbers of visits. Leading up to the Coronavirus pandemic in 2020, there were over 90 million visits per year, with all the benefits that brings to the nation's health and wellbeing. The economic value to the rural economy has been estimated at over four billion pounds per year. The advantages have to be balanced with the possible adverse effects, however. These can include degradation and erosion of the land and a strain on the local transport infrastructures. Another serious consequence is the effect on house prices and the ability of local families to buy into the housing market.

Our National Parks appear to be in relatively good health fifty years after John Hillaby's epic walk. If Dartmoor and Exmoor are being destroyed, it didn't seem obvious to me as I rode through. In the decades since *Journey through Britain*, the importance of issues such as environmental protection, economic sustainability, rural livelihoods, wildlife, cultural heritage, transport, biodiversity and affordable housing has been recognised. These are being given higher priority now in the management plans of each National Park.

The weather continued to be perfect and the views amazing. For no other reason than it was there, I struck out across the moors on the B3223 to Simonsbath, which is to Exmoor what Postbridge is to Dartmoor – the village in the middle of the moor. I headed south over the moors and crossed the River Exe close to its source. Exmoor is a giant dome of moorland, similar geologically to its big brother that I'd visited earlier in the day. Up on that stretch of road, I was traversing the top of the dome, under big skies across huge open expanses of upland heath, grassy moorland and blanket bog. It was getting warm and the road disappeared and reappeared on the horizon ahead of me, in a shimmering mirage. The place seemed deserted. I didn't even get a glimpse of the famous Exmoor ponies, the stocky little native breed that is thought to go back to Iron Age times. They are officially rare, with only a few hundred surviving these days, but wherever they were surviving, it was out of sight from the road I was on. Perhaps they'd gone to the beach for the day.

I didn't see any red deer either. There are up to 3,000 on Exmoor somewhere, the largest herd in England. They have inhabited the area for thousands of years and have been hunted for all that time. It's a bitterly controversial subject and one that John Hillaby discussed in his book, objectively stating the views of several people he met. The local population and the vast majority of the farming folk appear to support hunting. Their argument goes, as it did back in 1966, that if the deer aren't hunted, they will die out anyway. They claim that hunting is necessary and the most effective means of protecting the red deer population. People opposed to hunting claim that torturing and killing innocent wild animals is wrong, whether it's called sport or herd management. Stag-hunting was banned in England and Wales by the Hunting Act of 2004. Still, the Devon and Somerset Staghounds, founded in 1855, claims to meet three times a week in the season 'to manage the deer on behalf of the local farmers and landowners'. Enough said – it's a subject that will provoke strong views from both sides and the view from the outside will be different to that of the locals. I'll take the Hillaby approach of refraining from giving an opinion.

Simonsbath is an attractive little place that only really came into being in the 19th century. A small hamlet developed around the existing Simonsbath House, home of the Knight family. John Knight bought the now Grade II listed house in 1818. He was another visitor to the area from the Midlands, luckily a good few years before Aston Villa jerseys were considered a fashion item. This incomer was the son of a wealthy Shropshire ironmaster, presumably one of the first beneficiaries of the Industrial Revolution. John Knight and his successors did much to shape the Exmoor we see today. They enclosed the area with stone walling that still exists in long stretches, and they created several farms in the central part of the moor. Today in the village there is an inn, a hotel, a National Trust sawmill, tearooms and a car park from which many walks emanate. You can also find dog-friendly bars and rooms there – for anyone considering a Lynmouth/Simonsbath canine twin-centre holiday. I'm sure I wouldn't usually have noticed that; the Vincent experience must have affected me more than I thought.

I didn't want to miss any of the tremendous A39 route

across the top of Exmoor, so I retraced my tracks over some lonely moorland, back towards Lynmouth. It was such a lovely day and there was practically no one around. I took a few photos of myself cruising on the Royal Enfield across an exposed section of the moor. I set up the mini-tripod on the verge and fiddled about with the timer settings on my camera. I rode up and down a hundred yards of this quiet bit of road several times trying to get the timing right, so the camera took a picture just as I was riding past. I went completely bandit, as it was so deserted, and rode past without a motorcycle jacket or helmet. I reckoned it was safe enough at about 15 mph on an empty road. It took a few attempts before I appeared in the photo as anything other than a dot in the distance or missing altogether. Eventually, I was successful and got a decent picture. Even at that lethargic pace, it felt fantastic to have the wind in my hair and feel the sun through my T-shirt. In my mind, it was *The Great Escape* and I was a tanned Steve McQueen posing moodily yet magnificently as I cruised past on my Triumph TR6. If anyone had been unfortunate enough to come along and see me at that moment, I'm sure I must have looked more like a dishevelled Mr Bean. If there is any doubt in the minds of any concerned friends, relatives or law enforcement officers reading this, I just made that last bit up for a better read.

I re-joined the A39 back at Lynmouth and turned right towards Bridgwater. The road and views continued to delight. The route takes you through fertile farming country. Much of Exmoor is the product of thousands of years of farming. It results from woodlands being cleared, bogs drained, and vegetation controlled by grazing animals. Exmoor ponies have become so efficient at this job over the centuries that some have even been sent abroad recently to help others with the task. An initial vanguard of ponies, with notable grazing and conservation skills, was sent to the Czech Republic for scrub eating duties in one of their National Parks in 2015.

They were so successful at the job that more were posted overseas later the same year and more again in 2018.

A windswept tree on Exmoor

I continued eastwards on the A39 through to the tiny village of Porlock and on to Minehead for my overnight stop. This section of road is arguably the best of the South West's best. Along this stretch, you encounter Porlock Hill, reputably the steepest A-road in Britain, some sections of which have a 25 per cent gradient. Fortunately, I was going down it and glad I wasn't heading in the opposite direction stuck behind a line of caravans.

It was late afternoon by the time I arrived in Minehead and headed for the youth hostel, which is located on the southern outskirts of the town at the end of quite a long, unmade road. As with every other YHA hostel on my trip, the staff were super friendly and they let me park close to the building, even though the main car park was a little distance away. I got my gear into the hostel, checked out the evening meal options and tracked down a warm shower.

I feel compelled to give a big shout out to the YHA and its Scottish counterpart at this point. They've done such a fantastic job in England, Scotland and Wales since the 1930s, to encourage people of all ages to get out and enjoy the countryside and much more. I was told by one warden that the organisation got into dire financial straits after the Foot and Mouth epidemic of 2001 and many hostels were closed down. Apparently, the Emscott hostel that I stayed in on my way down to Cornwall was only saved because the local farmer bought it and then agreed to let the YHA run it. I hope things don't change too much and that they allow the original principles to prevail. Many of the hostels have a lovely old-fashioned atmosphere with comfy sofas, board games and libraries of books. I hope they stay that way and that as I progress into my sixties, my youth continues for a few years yet.

Over my dinner and a cold beer, I reflected on another fantastic day. That was two now. Surely, it would be impossible to maintain those levels of scenery, weather and crazy encounters. I have to report also that the lanes of Devon were every bit as good as the Cornish ones.

The florally decorated back lanes of Devon

Mile after mile of lovely spring flowers was a genuine treat, once again. The next day I would be out of the South West, around the corner and into the Wye Valley. I wondered if I could keep the geo-gastro theme going; I'd eaten a pasty in Cornwall, fudge in Devon – I needed to think of something suitable to eat in my stopover at Cheddar. I couldn't wait.

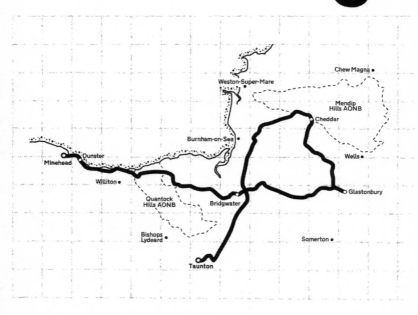

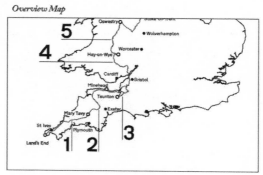

Overview Map

MINEHEAD TO TAUNTON

One of the best things about a road trip adventure like *Another Journey through Britain* is the random things that happen along the way, assuming they're nice random things. The first two days had already thrown up some memorable experiences; the incredible archaeological richness of west Cornwall, the raw beauty of Dartmoor and Vincent's hand-some mug, to name but three. As I was about to find out, however, the unexpected things that jump out at you aren't always welcome. Day three was another day of surprises, but it included one I could have done without.

I awoke early in Minehead Youth Hostel to another glorious day, but there were no unusual percussion instru-ments supporting the dawn chorus, as there had been the previous morning. After routine morning ablutions, I opted for the youth hostel cooked breakfast again. Why change a winning formula? And I didn't know when I'd be able to refuel again. This strategy followed a tried and tested one adopted by our beloved Welsh terrier over the years – if it's there, eat it.

My fellow breakfasting guests only numbered four, but there was a wider age range than I'd seen at the Penzance hostel. There was a middle-aged birdwatching couple, summer visitors from the Midlands, who'd flown south for a twitching week. Both looked at home in this semi-urban environment, feeding on titbits and seemingly tolerant of humans. The female had unusually bright plumage and squawked loudly. The male, less confident, had almost no plumage, scratched around busily for something to graze on and was a university professor. There was a mountain biker from Bournemouth, probably in his late twenties. Emerging from his shorts, his bruised and battered legs, boxer style, carried a reminder of every fall that had laid him down and cut him. I used the term 'morning ablutions' in our brief exchange of polite small talk over the toaster. His face went blank for a second and I wondered if he hadn't heard me or if he hadn't understood me. Then his face relaxed as he worked it out and he came back with: 'Oh the triple S, mate – shit, shave and shower'. How charming. The fourth member of the morning's breakfast club was a loud hillwalker from Wigan, about my age. If you can possibly stretch to it, think Brian Blessed with a George Formby accent. This tenuous link allows me to repeat an appropriate quote from the big fella with the booming voice: 'You can't call it an adventure unless it's tinged with danger. The greatest danger in life, though, is not taking the adventure at all'.

Once again, a lazy breakfast was an enjoyable time to pore over the maps, both to familiarise myself with the route ahead and to remind myself of suitable places to stop. At this point, I would normally chip in with something witty about never needing an excuse to look at maps. But perhaps I should mention the occasion back in the 1980s, when maybe even I took things a map sheet too far. I spent just over three years of my OS career updating the 1:50,000 Landranger maps. I was part of a team of twelve surveyors, and for most of that time, I travelled around Scotland, moving on every month to another area, updating the OS maps as I went. I remember going on a train journey from Inverness down to Edinburgh towards the end of my stint.

I was watching the world go by outside through the window in a bit of a daydream and for two or three seconds, I was seeing everything passing by as a 1:50,000 map... yellow minor roads, blocks of buildings, pylon lines... everything. I saw the map symbol equivalent of the real world. I was Keanu Reeves for a moment, looking at the raw digital file of our perceived world, *Matrix*-style. A neat trick looking back, but perhaps my brain was telling me to leave off the cartography crack for a while.

The map I was looking at in the hostel on *Another Journey through Britain,* day three, was a cheap UK road atlas I'd bought as part of my road trip preparations. I'd marked up my intended route with a yellow highlighter, along with some places I wanted to look at on the way. Some were locations where John Hillaby had stopped and others I chose just because they looked interesting and worth a visit. I browsed through the leaflets in the youth hostel dining area looking for further inspiration and came across a reference to what was, reputedly, the tallest tree in England. It was just a few miles from the hostel, so it was worth a small diversion. I suspect, like Arthur's Round Table, there could be several competing claims for the tallest tree in England, but obviously, the tree I was going to visit, planted back in the 1870s, was the genuine article. Having been to inspect it, I think the tree standing right next to it looked even higher, but it's difficult to tell when you're craning your neck to look up nearly 200 feet.

I came across the alleged record-breaker on the 'Tall Trees Trail' on the Dunster Estate, about four miles out of Minehead and a brief walk from the Forestry Commission's Nutcombe Bottom picnic site. For some reason, Tina Turner popped up on my cranium jukebox playlist. I heaved the bike up onto its stand in the picnic site car park and followed the signs to the trail. I didn't want the worry of leaving my panniers behind but wasn't sure how far the trail would take me. Despite the inconvenience, I took both panniers and my crash helmet along the path with me. It wasn't ideal, but I couldn't relax with all my worldly goods on display to anyone who happened upon the car park – not that there was any sign of anyone around that early in the morning. It reminded me of that famous philosophical mind puzzle; if you leave your panniers in a forest car park and no one is there to see them get nicked, were they really nicked?

It was a trail and there were lots of tall trees, so no Trade Description issues there. My expectation levels had been low, but the walk turned out to be far more enjoyable than I'd anticipated. The tallest tree in England would always be worth ticking off the list, which I readily admit is probably male compulsive behaviour. To be honest, that was about all I was hoping to do that morning. As I walked through the woodland grove, I noticed that it was having a calming effect. It was such a soothing and peaceful place. Plodding slowly along, like a packhorse with my two panniers and crash helmet, the sun filtered through the towering Douglas fir trees into shafts of golden light that fanned out over a soft carpet of needles on the forest floor. The trail took me alongside a small stream that chuckled away contentedly to itself and added to the air of calm. A touch of gentle harp accompaniment and I would have been in a woodland pine air-freshener advert.

Maybe our pagan ancestors, who worshipped trees, were on to something. There's a school of thought that says we should spend much more time in woodlands as an antidote to our modern obsession with smartphones and social media. Less screen time and more forest time could be the rallying cry of eco-psychology, an ideology that advocates a closer spiritual connection with nature. Its proponents point to current-day emotional problems in society and the need to reassert the human connection with our natural environment. We need to get out and breathe the forest air, smell the trees and feel the calmness of the woods. There's a growing body of evidence to prove the positive effects on mental health and the same applies to being near water or up in the mountains.

No surprise there for those of us who like to escape to the hills from time to time for a mental re-boot. The Japanese use the term Shinrin-Yoku, or forest bathing, to describe soaking up the atmosphere and mood of the forest as I was doing on the forest trail that morning. It seemed plausible to me, in that moment, to imagine a positive flow of energy in the same way that forests soak up our carbon dioxide and breathe out oxygen.

The Tall Trees Trail near Dunster

Maybe it was the fact that no one else was around, or perhaps it was a touch of Shinrin-Yoku, but I emerged from the woodlands feeling calm and content. Something was working. Maybe the Crown Estate, which manages the Dunster Estate, is missing a trick here. It could brand the Tall Trees Trail as a 'Therapy Thoroughfare' or 'Wellness Way' and invite visitors to dip their toes into some forest bathing. I wouldn't want too many people latching on to it, mind you, and the forest trail turning into a pedestrian procession like the one I'd seen at St Ives seafront.

I returned to the car park, heart rate and blood pressure suitably lowered, but glad to get rid of the panniers again. I floated serenely around the bike feeling super chilled and didn't want to do anything to upset the vibe. As I put the panniers back on the rear rack, I stressed that I might disturb the harmony of the energy flow around the bike, maybe risking the Feng Shui of my two wheels. I told myself I was overthinking it and fired up the engine.

I rode back towards the coast, down narrow Somerset lanes. Yet more delectable verges of tall and colourful spring flowers waved me through politely as I breezed by. I made my way a few miles northwards, still wrapped in the after-glow of my tranquil forest bathing session, to look around Dunster. The medieval village of Dunster has over 200 listed buildings and appears to have survived the ravages of time well preserved, unspoilt and in good shape. It was charm-ingly oldie-worldie and came complete with an ancient priory, dovecote, packhorse bridge, a castle and plenty of tearooms. It reminded me a lot of Chagford, which I'd visited the previous day, and although both have plenty of plus points, I think on balance Chagford got my vote. I had a nagging doubt about that, borne from a guilty feeling that once again I hadn't spent long enough looking around Dunster to do it justice. Even John Hillaby complained about not having enough time on his journey to wander around and talk to more people, and he was walking! Oh well, Dunster would have to be another place to mark down for the future, and my wife, Jan, would benefit later from my haste now. On my way out of town, I had a quick look at the impressive Dunster Castle, which stands imposingly on the skyline to the south of the village. By a quick look, I mean that I rode up the drive, turned around in the car park and rode out again. Too rushed once again.

I continued eastwards with a heavy heart at the thought of leaving Exmoor behind me but looking forward to seeing what discoveries lay ahead. Next up was Bridgwater, where, in 1966, John Hillaby noted that the main employer was a company called British Cellophane. The other two principal

employers in the town made 'brassieres' and radio compo-
nents. That's quite a heady mixture. I thought there should be
a snappy way of referring to these three essential industries;
there should be a Bridgwater equivalent of Dundee's pleas-
ingly rhythmical 'Jam, Jute and Journalism'. I spent a few
miles churning it over as I continued along the A39 eastwards, but the best I could manage was a disappointingly un-
rhythmic 'Wraps, Cups and Chips'.

The British Cellophane story is one that's been replicated
in many UK industries over the years as products have come
to the fore, become part of everyday life and then gradually
faded, being replaced by new products, cheaper alternatives
or new technology. Cellophane is the thin transparent sheet
used for food packaging or wrapping flowers. The company,
British Cellophane, set up production in Bridgwater in 1937
and was still employing 3,000 workers late into the 20th
century. The beginning of the end came as alternative and
more eco-friendly packaging materials were developed. The
Bridgwater plant eventually closed in 2005 and in 2012, the
French company, Électricité de France or EDF, which seems to
have a habit of going around building nuclear power stations
in the UK, bought the old British Cellophane site. Within
three years, EDF had levelled the old buildings. The site was
used to create temporary accommodation for workers
constructing the Hinkley Point C nuclear power station, about
eleven miles away as the white van drives. The construction
site was expected to be the biggest in Europe, – the size of a
small town – employing up to 4,500 workers. The locals
might miss the employment provided by the old cellophane
factory, but no one I met seemed to miss the stink the old
factory produced. Despite some diligent research on the spot
and after my LeJog ride, I never got to find out anything more
about the brassieres or radio parts to which John Hillaby
referred. There's only so much research you want to be doing
on bra factories; you don't know where your web search
engine might take you. 'Oh, that leather basque website,

Jan... funny how that popped up... I was just doing some research on Bridgwater'.

If John Hillaby was worried about the development of what he called 'water undertakings' on Dartmoor, I wonder what he would make of how our water supply and other UK infrastructures have changed over the last fifty years. When you live through those decades, you don't notice the gradual changes, except perhaps the privatisation explosion in the 1980s. But when you compare the situation in the mid-1960s with what we have now, the differences are profound. There has been a proliferation of organisations supplying water in England, Scotland and Wales. Delve into the complexities of who owns these organisations and the waters become muddy. Scotland and Northern Ireland still both receive their water supplies from state-controlled organisations (Scottish Water and Northern Ireland Water). In England and Wales, ten privatised utility companies manage both water and waste and fifteen provide drinking water. Most of them are in the hands of private equity and infrastructure funds, many with significant foreign shareholdings. Back in 1966, energy was the responsibility of a few large public institutions such as the National Coal Board, the Central Electricity Generating Board and British Petroleum. By 2018, we could buy our gas and electricity from over thirty different private companies, although most energy is currently supplied by a group known as 'the big six'. Of these, two are British and the other four are either French, German or Spanish. Ownership isn't always apparent: Scottish Power is a subsidiary of a Spanish company. Over 20 per cent of UK electricity comes from eight nuclear power plants, all owned and operated by the French company EDF, in which the French government has a majority shareholding.

Apart from the ownership aspects, another difference that has taken place over the years concerns the types of energy used. Coal was the number one source for our power stations back in the 1960s, providing over 80 per cent of the country's requirements. Even the trains were running on the stuff in those days. Nowadays, the proportion of electricity generated by coal is less than 5 per cent, mostly imported from Russia. The good news story is renewable energy. The percentage of electricity coming from wind and solar power has gone from zero back in the 1960s to nearly 40 per cent today, and the percentage is growing rapidly. The world's largest offshore wind farm is humming away in the North Sea. Before long, the fuel that stoked the fires of the Industrial Revolution will become history. Except for a few old nostalgic miners, most people will see that as a good thing.

Post and phones were the responsibility of the General Post Office at the time of John Hillaby's walk. Landline communication is now managed by the UK company, BT Group, while mobile communication is dominated by two British and two foreign-owned networks. Britain's two biggest airports, Heathrow and Gatwick, are now both operated by UK companies under foreign ownership. Back in 1966, the entire national rail network was managed by a state-owned company called the British Railways Board. It's more complicated now. Railway tracks and other infrastructures are the responsibility of Network Rail, which describes itself as a public company answerable to the government. Trains are run by many separate rail franchises. These are operated by a mixture of UK and foreign companies, many of which are wholly or partly owned by the governments of France, Germany, Spain and Italy.

Some people argue that these key communications, energy and transport services are pillars of the UK industrial infrastructure and are so important they should remain under government supervision. Things have transformed since the 1960s, but there is still considerable government control – it's just that it's no longer the UK government in control.

The next part of the journey again took me away from John Hillaby's original route. He skirted around Exmoor, visited Bridgwater and then headed over the Somerset Levels to Cheddar. He considered Somerset to be one of the most walker friendly counties he travelled through. I'm guessing that had a lot to do with the fact that vast expanses of it are flat and if I had just walked over Cornwall and Devon, I'm sure I'd appreciate walking on the flat for a while.

My route would be broadly similar to John Hillaby's original one, but the temptation to divert to Glastonbury, especially on such a glorious day, was too much. I continued to avoid the major roads and took more florally decorated lanes in search of 'Avalon'. The songs being selected by my cranium jukebox auto-switched to Roxy Music.

The town of Glastonbury, which had a New Age feel, was bathed in sunshine when I arrived in the late morning. I did a slow circuit of the town centre, somehow resisting the temptation to stock up on crystals, swords and medieval cloaks and found the small lane that runs up towards the Tor. Once again, I had the panniers issue – should I risk leaving them on the bike for a few minutes or haul them up to the top of the Tor and back? I took the risk of going without them this time but felt uneasy doing so. I parked in the lane right next to the gate to the shortish path that leads to St Michael's Tower on the summit of the Tor. I tucked the bike right up against the hedge to avoid causing any obstruction, although the double yellow lines in the lane hinted that I shouldn't technically have parked there. Again, this is something I've dreamt up after the event to embellish an otherwise dull story. It makes my story sound more like the two fingers to authority rantings of a badass biker rather than the mumblings of a curmudgeonly old geezer.

It's a five-minute stroll without panniers up to the top of the Tor, the one-time home of Gwyn ap Nudd, the mythological king of the fairies. The Tor and the tower are steeped in legend, with many exotic theories about King Arthur, Guinevere, the Holy Grail and the Isle of Avalon. When I reached the top, I took off my jacket and sat down for a few minutes to rest and soak up some mystical ley-line vibes. An eclectic, even eccentric, mix of people surrounded me. Before I set off on my ride, I wondered if I would come across the rich variety of characters that John Hillaby met on his walk. Would I still find those quirky diamonds? I needn't have worried; they seemed to pop up everywhere.

Glastonbury Tor

As I sat next to the tower on the Tor, two very fit looking runners in sweaty blue vests and Lycra shorts jogged rapidly on the spot right next to me, determined to keep running while they admired the view. I guessed the couple were probably in their late twenties. A giggly party of six teenage girls sat nibbling at a picnic on a carefully smoothed out tartan rug. Occasionally one would break off from the conversation to catch up with her social media updates before reporting back to the others, upon which they would all fall about in hysterical laughter. 'Oh, that Jeremy, he's such a muppet!' As befitted the location, there were several groups of hippy types featuring much orange and yellow baggy clothing. An energetic Ben Fogle lookalike was throwing juggling clubs alarmingly high into the Somerset sky. He was almost in control. There would occasionally be a loud rumble as the clubs all landed, followed by a slight pause while bystanders edged away, and the juggler's exclusion zone widened out a few more metres. There were two bare-chested old gents in shorts, with mahogany skins two sizes too big, who for some unaccountable reason I assumed to be locals. They looked like they were away with the king of the fairies, to be honest, but fair play, those were impressive tans for late May. I felt distinctly overdressed by comparison, with my heavy biker jeans and jacket.

I had forgotten just how good the views were from the Tor, although they should be fantastic with those vast expanses of flat Somerset Levels stretching out to the horizon. I loved the feel of the place. Just like the forest walk in the morning, the Tor had a kind of magic. No surprise at all that my internal jukebox instantly selected the title track from the 1986 Queen album.

Although I could have carried on people-watching for hours, I didn't want to hang around too long. This was partly because of the panniers, partly because of my parking arrangements and partly because of the Tor legend suggesting its role as a gateway to the Land of the Dead. At my age, you don't want to be hanging around such expiration portals any longer than you have to. I needed to get back to make sure the panniers were safe before I felt the Reaper's icy hand on my shoulder. If someone had left their bike on double yellow lines, that would also have been a concern. I took a few photos and set off down the path.

A very old woman with a stick was approaching the summit. She too was somewhat overdressed, as elderly people often are, and she was almost bent double with her exertions. I nodded a respectful acknowledgement and said a brief hello, not wanting to engage her in conversation for fear of her using up too much of her valuable breath. Good on her, I thought, admiring her spirit and hoping she'd not heard about those gateway rumours. After passing the old lady, I continued down the gravel path, passing another three groups of people on the way. The three snippets of conversation I heard as I walked past went like this. Firstly: 'I told him it wouldn't work, but he kept turning it till he completely stripped the bloody thread; it's bloody useless now'. Secondly: 'And that's why the whole concept of feminism is flawed and has to be totally rejected'. And lastly: 'Well, I bought a shed from them once, like the one we used in Zimbabwe for the toilet'. Speculating on those snapshots of other people's lives kept me amused for the rest of the walk back to the bike.

I got those pearls of wisdom written pronto in my notebook as soon as I reached the bike, without thinking any more about the implications for DIY, garden storage or women's rights. To be honest, I was more relieved to see that the bike and panniers were all still safely where I'd left them, and the windscreen was unencumbered by additional paperwork. I fired up the bike and set off again, northwards now towards Cheddar and some lunch.

Everything was going so much better than I could have dreamt. It had taken me two days to get down to Land's End from Oswestry and now on the third full day of the LeJog trip, well into my fifth day of riding, I was relaxing and enjoying myself. The initial anxieties of getting to Land's End, getting used to long days on the bike and wondering if I had the right kit had all just about vanished. I was now enjoying the steady daily routine of working my way up the country, stopping to see beautiful places and meeting interesting people. And so far, I'd been lucky enough to ride under glorious blue skies.

I feel that Cheddar punches above its weight. With a population of fewer than 6,000, it's only really a sizeable village, not much bigger than the Hinkley Point C power station construction site, yet the name Cheddar is known around the world. I wonder how many other small English villages can claim that. Its nearby neighbour Wells isn't much bigger, but it calls itself a city! It does, however, have a magnificent cathedral and a unique moated Bishop's Palace in its favour. Where Cheddar gets the added oomph, however, is from two globally famous names – the Cheddar Gorge and Cheddar cheese. I was looking forward to seeing the iconic landscape of the gorge again after lunch, which I was hoping would involve the other famous name. Traditionally, cheese has to be made within thirty miles of Wells Cathedral to earn the prestigious label 'Cheddar'. To be pedantic, Cheddar cheese is not one of the UK's protected cheese names, but West Country Farmhouse Cheddar is. The earliest references to Cheddar cheese go back to the 12th century. One story suggests that a milkmaid left her bucket of milk in the caves at Cheddar only to find a whole new product developing in the bucket when she came back. That product now accounts for over 50 per cent of total cheese sales in the UK and is the second favourite cheese consumed in the USA. Enough cheesy facts. Back to the ride.

I pulled into Cheddar just after 1 pm, to misquote one of my favourite *Easy Rider* songs, and stopped off at the Riverside Inn. The barman's lips broke into the faintest of smiles when I asked if the ploughman's lunch came with Cheddar cheese. Maybe the smile was more of a grimace – I think he'd heard that one before.

With my lunchtime salad, the geo-gastro hat trick was complete (Cheddar cheese added to my Cornish pasty and Devon fudge), and I swaggered off to the pub's beer garden to wallow in my achievement. The inn's car park contained quite a few camper vans; it seemed to be a favourite stopover spot for tourers. The beer garden was extensive and busy, as it should have been on such a lovely afternoon. It sloped down to a babbling stream, and in one corner there was a large kids' play area, also babbling, with kids of all sizes. I took out my dog-eared copy of *Journey through Britain* and read the section where the great man talks about this part of his walk. He seemed to visit a lot of pubs on the way. They were very much the preserve of workingmen in those days, somewhere a chap could slake his thirst after a hard day's graft. Nowadays, it was different, and the Riverside Inn was another reminder of how things have changed, with food and children's entertainment high on the list of priorities. The place was very family-orientated, and the families seemed to like the formula. Over an enjoyable lunch, I wondered how I could keep my geo-gastro theme going over the next couple of days; maybe some Somerset cider and then some cheese on toast when I arrived in Wales?

I got back on the bike, looking forward to unleashing a throaty roar of exhaust to echo around the confines of the gorge just up the road. I put the satnav on, and departed – get those earplugs ready, people of Cheddar!

Ah, wait a second, something doesn't feel right. Oh, shit, the rear tyre is as flat as a pancake.

My heart sank and I mentally went through a score of scenarios in fast forward for how the rest of the day might pan out – none of them ending well and all of them involving a significant change of schedule. Had I upset the Feng Shui of the bike with my careless repositioning of the panniers after the forest trail? Once again, I had to check myself. Good grief, no one had been hurt, a puncture wouldn't be terminal for the bike; I just had to get it repaired. I had a careful look for something obvious sticking out of the tyre but couldn't see anything. I didn't have a pump – of course.

There was no sign of a garage up or down the road, so I asked around. It turned out there was one on the way out of the village, so I rode off gingerly, hoping not to do any more damage. Seconds later, I limped into the garage, which luckily appeared only a hundred or so yards away from the inn. I threw myself at their mercy. The chap there put some air in the tyre, but it immediately hissed out again. I wasn't sure what was more deflated: the tyre or me. I was in a car garage and I was told that the tyre needed to be repaired properly at a motorcycle garage or else replaced. The Cheddar garage people were very helpful and rang around to find somewhere suitable for me, but without success.

Prompted by a 100 per cent lack of mechanical knowledge, I had had the foresight before the ride to arrange breakdown insurance and now seemed the time to unleash that backup plan. A customer in the garage advised me to park my broken bike over on the opposite side of the road because the breakdown assistance companies sometimes object to picking people up from a garage. Fair enough, so I scooted over the road and parked on a wide bit of kerb right outside Hansford's Deli. If anyone is considering potential locations in Cheddar to have a vehicle breakdown, this would be my top tip. The lovely ladies in the deli were very hospitable and provided me with somewhere to sit, refreshing drinks, a socket to charge my phone and a friendly chat... I was almost glad to have broken down.

My pleasant afternoon natter was rudely interrupted after about an hour, when the breakdown truck arrived. The amiable driver soon had my bike winched up on the back of the truck, but he then asked me a tricky question. 'Where do you want to go?' That threw me a bit. I'd assumed he would have a mental database of all the garages and repair facilities within a fifty-mile radius and would automatically take me to the nearest place that could get the job done. Nope. So, we spent the next half an hour ringing around again, trying to find a suitable garage to either mend or replace the tyre. You wouldn't think it would be that difficult, would you? The driver was casting his net in an ever-widening circle, and by the time the net reached Taunton, we struck lucky. There was a Royal Enfield dealer there and they could get me back on the road first thing tomorrow morning! I thought I could settle for that as it was already late afternoon, and it was unlikely that I'd find anyone else. In reality, I had no choice.

The rest of that day's journey wasn't as scenic as the first part. I had swapped meandering along the flower-scented back lanes of Somerset for a blast down the M5. As we drove south-west, back the way I'd come, I supplied the driver with brief verbal prompts every five minutes or so, and he related his life story as a rescue man. I should have known it, but he too was a Midlander and continuing a now-familiar theme, he also appeared to have worked his way through the full catalogue of tattoos from his local artist until they'd exhausted all visible skin surface. I thought about this. Back in 1966, when John Hillaby did his walk, I was twelve years old. I wasn't monitoring the phenomenon carefully, but my impression was that tattoos were only seen on the arms of men who stoked boilers in Her Majesty's Navy, train engine drivers, and maybe the occasional bus conductor. And anyway, I always assumed the latter two must be retired naval stokers.

For those not old enough to know, bus conductors were bus company uniformed employees who travelled on the bus, collected fares, issued tickets and told irresponsible lads to stop larking around. The conductors I remember were all men, normally had half a fag on the go and were experts in precision whistling. In the winter, they wore fingerless gloves. They weren't averse to chucking disrespectful schoolboys off the bus if required, and sometimes even if not required. Tattoos were relatively discreet as I recall, and normally involved anchors, bluebirds, or possibly endearing messages involving a mum, wife or girlfriend. Nowadays tattoos seem to be everywhere – on young mums pushing buggies, middle-aged dads showing their football allegiances and teenage girls swigging pints. It probably has a lot to do with overpaid footballers and the rise of the celebrity culture. I'm in danger of coming across all old geezer here, so I should balance things up by pointing out the positive aspects such as shops providing valuable employment, the creative outlet for many artists and people being able to express their personal individuality.

Anyway, back to my ride to Taunton, my driver multi-tasked impressively, for a man, as he juggled his attention between his life story, the road, his office and a stream of phone calls from an attention-seeking daughter. An hour later we arrived safely in Taunton and the driver then showed precocious manoeuvring skills by reversing his vehicle down a road that appeared slightly narrower than the truck itself, to park right outside the Royal Enfield dealer. I could never have pulled off that feat of driving. Job done and I was very grateful, thank you very much.

The people at GV Bikes couldn't have been more friendly, and they deserve a hearty round of applause for keeping *Another Journey through Britain* on the road. They had the right tyre for my bike and although they were busy, they promised to get me on my way first thing next morning, so my adventure wouldn't be seriously derailed. Fantastic. I made two rapid phone calls – one to cancel my campsite in the Wye Valley for that evening and the second to book a room in Taunton for the night. Good, I just had to get to Taunton Travelodge then. After a brief discussion, the lads from the garage agreed where the motel was and one of them offered to take me there on the pillion seat of his 1500cc Kawasaki. It was a colossal beast, the motorbike that is – a bit of a Chopper-style bike in the Harley Davidson mould. It was a fantastic-looking machine and sitting on it was like reclining into a big soft sofa – one that travels at 100 mph. To avoid doubt, we hardly touched a third of that speed. I decanted a few overnight essentials into a single pannier bag, swung my leg over the pillion seat of the Kawasaki and prepared for my knuckles to turn white. If you can imagine the scene from *Easy Rider* where Jack Nicholson sticks his golden football helmet on and rides off down the freeway on the back of Captain America's chopper bike... well, it was nothing like that.

We turned up at the location where everyone had agreed we would find the Travelodge. It was the Holiday Inn. Ah, no problem. My chauffeur knew where it must be and we roared off again around the ring-road to the right place, me snarling menacingly at trembling commuters on their way home in an uncalled-for display of biker badassery. In reality, I was just hanging on, and any snarling was my attempt to breathe through clenched teeth. My safe delivery was such a kind and generous gesture and my hero thundered away for his evening meal, while I checked into the Travelodge. I'd ridden just over 75 miles of my intended route and ended up about 25 miles from where I'd started! John Hillaby would have managed more than that walking... oh well, I was having an adventure, not a race.

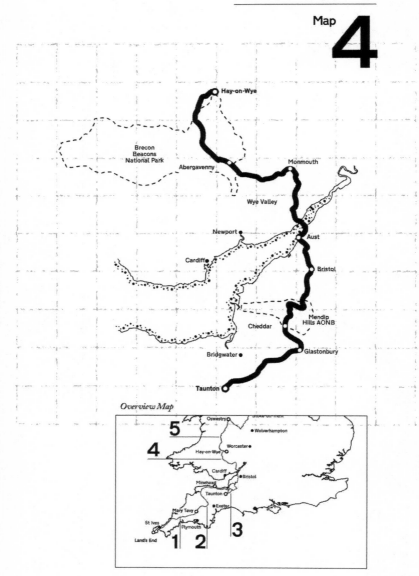

Brecon Beacons National Park

Hay-on-Wye

Abergavenny

Monmouth

Wye Valley

Newport

Aust

Cardiff

Bristol

Mendip Hills AONB

Cheddar

Bridgwater

Glastonbury

Taunton

Overview Map

5

4

Oswestry

Stoke-on-Trent

Wolverhampton

Hay-on-Wye

Worcester

Cardiff

Bristol

Minehead

Taunton

Exeter

St Ives

Mary Tavy

Plymouth

Land's End

1

2

3

TAUNTON TO HAY-ON-WYE

So far, my overnight stops had been an inn, two youth hostels and now a motel. I admit the latter had been comfortable and the inn was luxurious, but the youth hostels had quirkiness and charm and felt more like a proper adventure. My dawn chorus on day four was the gentle rumble of traffic as the commuters of Taunton travelled to work. This wasn't the stuff of road trip dreams but given my situation at about 2 pm yesterday, I'd take it. I was pleased to be getting back on my way again and returning to the LeJog route I'd planned. I'd soon be back on the highway, looking for adventure and whatever came my way.

The summer of 2018 is one that will go down in history as the joint hottest on record in the UK and for the first three days of my journey, I had enjoyed glorious weather with blue skies and sunshine all the way. It hadn't been too hot; it was just about perfect. Paranoid about the weather, as usual, I anxiously awaited the morning forecast on day four to see if my luck would continue. The weather map on BBC TV that morning showed the UK almost completely clear of cloud. Nice – except for a band of heavy rain and thunder that ran across South Wales, over the Taunton Travelodge, along the M4 and into Sussex. It looked like they expected the rain to move north-westwards up along the Welsh Borders at about the same speed as a Royal Enfield. You have to take these things in your stride. At least I was on my way again and I reckoned if I was lucky, I might just stay ahead of the northern edge of that band of wet weather.

The morning's events could hardly be described as a thrill-a-minute, or travel memoir gold. To tell it how it was, I popped over the road from the hotel to a Sainsbury's super-store to enjoy another cooked breakfast. A supermarket on the Taunton bypass – good grief, it was some epic journey. On the positive side, however, I was refuelled with a Sainsbury's five-item Big Breakfast, and hopefully, my motorbike awaited me.

I got a taxi from the hotel and arrived at GV Bikes just as the last checks were being done after the tyre-fitting and test ride. I loaded up, paid up and was back on the road again (Canned Heat already cued up on the turntable). Game on!

Although the skies were looking distinctly leaden, it still hadn't rained and I pushed on back to Cheddar, determined to hear that roar from the bike echoing around the Cheddar Gorge. I stopped briefly to show off my fully inflated tyre to the ladies of the deli, who somehow managed to contain their excitement and while I was there, I picked up a slice of Bakewell tart for later.

It didn't take long to get to the gorge and just as I entered the great chasm, the first spots of rain hit the surface of the B3135, pitter-patting some mocking applause at my late arrival. I stopped as soon as the opportunity arose and got my wet weather gear on; I didn't want to leave it until it was too late. That seemed to do the trick; the rain stopped as quickly as it had started.

The spectacular Cheddar Gorge was created when melt-waters carved through Carboniferous limestone at the end of the Ice Age. It looked very dramatic under dark and threat-ening skies as I entered. Maybe it looked even better in that menacing mood than in bright sunshine... was what I tried to convince myself. The ride through the Cheddar Gorge lasts for a couple of impressive twisty miles, with the cliffs towering 400 feet above the road. I took it slowly to appreciate the view and I remembered to get some throaty engine roars in. There didn't seem to be anyone else around to appreciate them. OK then, onwards to Bristol and the River Severn.

The towering cliffs of Cheddar Gorge

The ride north from the Cheddar Gorge and around Chew Valley was pleasant enough, through undulating arable and dairy countryside, but I think I was becoming too preoccupied with the skies to admire my surroundings properly. Was it or wasn't it going to rain? The weather was in that indecisive in-between mood; it would spit with rain for a few minutes, and I'd think, 'Right, here we go; this is serious', and then it would ease off and stop again.

As I approached Bristol, still keeping to minor roads and lanes, the scenery morphed from rural to urban. It was changing for the worse. For my LeJog journey so far, I'd been immersed in rural England (well, if we skip over the M5 and Taunton bypass). Now I was riding through suburbia and into the fringes of an enormous city. I hadn't been used to a big urban environment for a few days and it felt like the gloomy surroundings were matching the weather. I was going from quiet, sunny lanes to dark grey streets. I was already looking forward to getting out the other side and back into the countryside again. That would not be for a little while yet, though. I had to negotiate Bristol and get over the Severn Bridge before I could enjoy the delights of the beautiful Wye Valley.

When it comes to vehicle maintenance, there are two types of people. Those who do and those who don't. People like my big brother, Bill, need no real excuse to dismantle a vehicle and rebuild it again. If you wait too long at the lights, he's likely to whip out a toolbox and adjust something. Modern cars have increasingly sophisticated electronics, computerised this, that and the other, and advanced engine management systems. That's not a problem for Bill because he doesn't have a modern car. His two vehicles are old ones – proper ones where you can spring valves, bleed nipples and tap rockers – whatever all that means.

My philosophy has always been if it ain't broke, don't fix it. For me, a vehicle is a means of getting from A to B. It's something to enable an adventure, but I don't want the adventure of messing around with it. It's the same with my Classic Royal Enfield. I love the retro look and delight with feigned nonchalance at the admiring glances, but I want to use the motorcycle to go places. Someone else can do the servicing and maintenance. Which makes my decision to stop on my way through Bristol to check the bike's rear tyre pressure on day four bewildering. What was I thinking? The tyres had only just been tested that morning by someone who knew what they were doing!

Anyone who knows me would recognise this as uncharacteristic behaviour. Maybe the stress of yesterday's puncture was messing with my head. Anyway, I pulled into a filling station forecourt somewhere on my way into Bristol and parked the bike next to the air machine. First, I had to get a

50p coin from the shop. You'd have thought the shock of spending that much money for air would have been enough to shake me out of the madness. Next, I had to take the dust cap off the rear tyre and put it somewhere where I'd find it again. So far, so good; I was in the moment and thinking about what I was doing – albeit not why. Pressure set, money in the machine, off we go. Except the pesky nozzle on the airline wouldn't snap over the tyre valve like it's supposed to – like it would do, if I was a mechanic. Air hissed out of both the tyre and the airline dramatically, like a standoff between two angry and highly pressurised cobras. In horror, I quickly whipped the airline nozzle off the valve again. Great, now the tyre was definitely not at the right pressure, and I'd just made things worse. Two more efforts like that and the tyre was nearly flat.

Jesus, why did I think this was such a wonderful idea?! My live commentary switched to base Anglo Saxon for a few seconds as I tried to force the airline nozzle onto the valve from different angles. Each time the bike chain, mudguard or some other stupid bloody thing impeded a proper docking manoeuvre. On my last attempt, before ripping a branch off a tree to give the bike a damn good Basil Fawlty style thrashing, I got a good tight fit, and the air went surging into the tyre. Thank God for that! I waited for the air machine readout to show the correct pressure, then waited longer and then longer still, just in case. I removed the airline and inspected the scene for damage. I had oil and grease all over both hands, over both wrists and a good distance up my right arm. I'd cut one finger and with the blood mingling elegantly with the oil and grease, I could have entered my right arm for the Turner Prize.

Well, that went well, didn't it? I was just so relieved that I had at least eventually got the air in. I sat on the kerb, feeling very Mr Bean-like. I broke into a cold sweat at the thought of what had nearly happened – having to ring up the breakdown people again to tell them I had another flat tyre. I eventually cleaned myself up in the garage washroom, relieving the paper towel machine of all its contents, topped the bike up with fuel and rode on again. I'd had such a brilliant start to the LeJog adventure and then in two days, I'd had a flat tyre almost twice, once of my own doing. I felt stupid and vowed to reaffirm my long-standing vehicle maintenance mantra once again. After all – it hadn't been broke.

Bristol hustled and bustled and felt like hostile territory after several days of meandering through the quiet country lanes of south-west England. I was happy when I was out the other side of the city and heading towards the Severn crossing. My route plan allowed for a brief stop at the village of Aust on the south bank of the River Severn, right between the two motorway bridges. John Hillaby had crossed the river there by ferry in 1966 before construction of the first bridge had been completed. Like Cheddar, the tiny village of Aust seems to have gained greater recognition than its size would suggest. Mentioned in the Domesday Book, Aust was one end of a Roman road that led to Cirencester. John Hillaby reminded his readers that it was the place where St Augustine crossed into Wales. He also mentioned that Aust has a particular reputation amongst geologists for the fossils found in its red and white cliffs of mudstone and limestone.

It took me a while, but I eventually found the place where John Hillaby crossed the river for one shilling, accompanied by twelve cars and a furniture van. When I finally stumbled across the old ferry terminal site, I found a lot of the old building and jetty remaining, although it was long abandoned, overgrown and neglected.

Taking an imaginary ticket from the old ticket office turnstile that was still in place, I wandered down to what was left of the pier. The skeletal wooden remains still cross the mudflats before collapsing wearily into the River Severn. It wasn't hard to imagine the vehicles queuing up and boarding the ferry, a maximum of nineteen at a time, for the short journey over to Beachley on the north bank of the river. The trip saved going sixty miles by road via Gloucester. Back in 1966, the ferry had another famous visitor. Bob Dylan turned up to promote Martin Scorsese's *No Direction Home* film. In the photos, you can see the Severn Bridge being built in the background.

The old ferry pier at Aust

Two other visitors were quietly looking around the old ferry site at the same time as me that morning. I assumed the older of the two men was the dad and he seemed to be telling his son about the old days. I overheard him talking about the 'Severn Princess', the last ferry to operate on the route. The boat was being restored by local heritage enthusiasts. I mooched around the site for a while longer, still calming down after the second tyre incident, with my cranium jukebox now providing a medley of moody Dylan tracks in my head. A slice of Bakewell tart lifted my spirit, but what I really needed was to get into the wooded Wye Valley for some more Shinrin-Yoku. I bade farewell to Aust, looked up anxiously at the darkening clouds and thought to myself – 'A Hard Rain's A-Gonna Fall'.

I rode on, over a blustery River Severn and onto Chepstow

and Wales, convinced that the rain was imminent. My route followed the A466 up the Wye Valley and over the Black Mountains towards Hay-on-Wye, which was my stop for the night. I was still following John Hillaby's route, more or less, and picking off the landmarks he mentioned along the way. I was relaxing again, encouraged by how I seemed to be missing the rain and bathing in the Shinrin-Yoku oozing from the oaks, beeches and limes of the lower Wye Valley.

Even when the sun isn't shining, I love that bit of road. You can't go fast; it demands a slow meander, mostly through a tunnel of towering trees. Now and again there's a glimpse of the swirling waters of the Wye River or the bright green floodplain. Before long, I'd arrived in Tintern and as always, the remains of the old Cistercian abbey looked proud and magnificent, despite the best efforts of Henry VIII to trash the place back in 1536. This was one he decided to leave in ruins, just to remind everyone that he was more powerful than the Church. I stopped for a while, if for no other reason than it's just a beautiful place to be, and while I was there, it would have been rude not to try some fruity Welsh teacake and a pot of tea for one. Ah, that's more like it.

Still wary of those grey skies, I rode up through the rest of the Wye Valley to Monmouth and then up to Abergavenny, via a short blast along 'Highway A41 Revisited' – to squeeze in another very tenuous Dylan link. Heading northwards through the Brecon Beacons National Park, I was soon into spectacular mountain scenery. The Bristol airline fiasco was soon a fast-fading nightmare as I cruised into and across the Black Mountains. My route took me via Crickhowell and Talgarth, through rolling old red sandstone moorland, boasting a regularly spaced covering of scraggy looking sheep. The ride over the hills to Talgarth was another one of those bikers' delights; it had just the right bend mixture, switching one way and the other so you can gently lean the bike rhythmically from side to side. The Mullion Missile might have been at home here, but he would probably have been averaging about 30 mph faster than my gentle cruise – with his shoulders in the hedge. It was relaxing and I breezed along, admiring the view and reflecting on how I seemed to be back on track again after yesterday's slight hiccup.

While maintaining 100 per cent concentration on my riding, my thoughts skipped around randomly from route planning, jobs to do at home, the night's stopover and the fragile nature of Southampton Football Club's defence. As if to confirm my re-established state of relaxation, I treated the upland sheep and a few crows to an unlikely medley of musical classics including 'Bohemian Rhapsody', 'Nessun Dorma', 'The Logical Song' and 'Sunshine on Leith'. At least no animals were knowingly harmed in that non-musical interlude.

When I was doing my route planning during the first few months of the year, I spotted that the 2018 Hay-on-Wye Literary Festival was due to begin when I was expecting to pass through the area. So, I incorporated a visit as part of my adventure. Just as well really because having a stopover planned for Hay-on-Wye meant I had prepared for a short day four ride… which meant I could catch up on my schedule after yesterday's pneumatic let down. What brilliant foresight. I was making for Hay, even though the sun wasn't shining. And I had a festival to visit and a gig to go to!

Best of all, my accommodation for the night would be a yurt. A yurt (Russian) or ger (Mongolian) is in effect a substantial family-sized and portable tent. They have been used for thousands of years by nomadic people on the steppe of Central Asia, especially in Mongolia. The traditional style is a felt-lined round structure with head height vertical walls supporting a roof of straight poles that lead up to a central crown. I've been in the genuine thing on the plains of Mongolia. With little wood-burning stoves, they are cosy even in sub-zero temperatures, but they can also keep their occupants cool in sweltering summers. They seem to be very popular in Britain now on the glamping circuit, for campsites and festivals. I arrived at Hay-on-Wye, still dry, by late afternoon. I found the festival campsite and checked in.

There was a sizeable grass-covered field that was acting as a festival car park and despite not appearing to have a dedicated motorcycle area, it did at least have 24-hour security. I put the bike up on its stand in a large gap between two cars and hauled the panniers off the bike yet again. I went to check in and find my yurt. A brief walk and there it was – on the edge of the encampment, with a little luggage tag flapping in the breeze showing its number.

Luxury camping at Hay-on-Wye

It looked like the Mongolians had arrived ahead of me and packed about a hundred yurts tightly together to stop the wolves from getting to the horses – good thinking in these parts of Wales. There was no door, just a square of canvas to roll up, but once inside, it was great. The yurt I had for the night was a relatively small one – a compact two-person job, but lovely and snug inside. It had a mattress, sheets and rugs, a little cupboard and a light. This was luxury camping. I got changed and set off for the bright lights of Hay-on-Wye, just as the first pitter-patter of that band of rain arrived. After a day of close encounters, the rain had finally caught up with me and although I didn't realise this at the time, it was to hang around for the next 24 hours.

Anyone going to Hay-on-Wye looking for an enjoyable read will not be disappointed. It's said to be the world's largest second-hand and antiquarian book centre. After you've wandered around the place for a while, you realise that it is not, as you first thought, a picturesque market town – you are actually inside a giant library where they have streets instead of aisles between the bookshelves. Even if you're not a book lover, the place has a lot to offer. It has charming shops, pubs and restaurants, a river and no less than two Norman castles dating back to the times when Hay-on-Wye was the front line in a succession of battles between the local English nobles and their rival Welsh kings. The relatively small population of around 2,000 somehow copes with over 250,000 visitors at the time of the annual literary festival. There is also a music and philosophy festival held at the same time now. I hadn't been to the festival before, so this was my chance to tick another experience box. Three interesting Hay-on-Wye facts for you: it's twinned with Timbuktu in Mali. Second, it was in Hay that the late singer-songwriter Ian Dury wrote the lyrics '…from the gardens of Bombay, all the way to lovely Hay'. Third, Bill Clinton described the 2001 literary festival as 'The Woodstock of the mind'. He always had a way with words.

I soon found my way to the festival site and explored. The bulk of the event was taking place within a large tented village. They had subdivided the undercover area into sections, with spaces for book readings, discussions, eating, drinking, musical performances, a BBC broadcasting studio and quite a few more books. Once again, I was mingling with an eclectic mix, but these people seemed, in a very sweeping generalisation, to belong in either the literary or agricultural pigeonholes – or bookshelves. There were hundreds of people mingling and chatting, eating, drinking, reading and having a splendid time. I found an enormous food tent and walked around for a couple of circuits to assess what was on offer. Every culinary category you could wish for seemed available and I settled for a Thai vegetarian curry and a beer. I fished out my festival tickets to ponder the rest of the evening.

My entertainment choice couldn't have been much more diverse. First up was a talk by Minette Batters, the first female President of the National Farmers' Union, followed by a gig by the singer Jake Bugg. Both turned out to be brilliant in their own ways, the second being more of a foot-tapper than the first. A talk by Minette Batters in the programme of events explained why there were masses of farmers and young farmers on display. The former typically appeared in twos or threes, wearing green wellies, lots of tweed, waistcoats, checked shirts and flat caps. The latter were mostly younger versions of the former, appeared in larger herds, were very excitable and often alcohol fuelled. There was a touch of the rustic hipster look on show with some of the young farmer chaps – denim replacing tweed for the trousers, lots of padded down waistcoats, well-sculpted facial hair and upmarket wellies.

The only two snippets of conversation that I overheard – and remembered well enough to write down later – were both like extracts from *The Archers*. The first, in a rustic Eddie Grundy type accent, went: 'Bloody useless; the lambs were lucky to make two quid'. The second, in a posher Brian Aldridge accent, went: 'Yes but the verges are looked after by the council now you know. The only trees left growing are those right next to the telegraph poles'. I took these to be representative summaries of the current economic and environmental situation in the agricultural sector and felt well prepared to listen to the presentation by Minette Batters.

Her talk took the form of an interview, followed by questions from the floor. She came across as very knowledgeable and an excellent communicator. It left me wondering why it had taken 110 years for the National Farmers' Union to get around to finding a woman to be their president. The interviewer ploughed through a quick-fire range of questions covering Brexit, the government's environment strategy, 'cheap' food, drone technology, soil quality and much more. As he did so, my mind wandered back again to 1966 and how things had changed since John Hillaby's walk. Although the number of agricultural workers nowadays has just about halved from around 400,000 in 1966, approximately 70 per cent of the total UK land area is still used for agriculture. To varying degrees, our urban areas have encroached into the surrounding countryside and we have lost swathes of land to the motorway network, but I think anyone who walks or travels the LeJog route today still experiences a mainly rural landscape. Green belt policy and the creation of National Parks and AONB have helped. Back in the 1960s, there still existed a degree of the post-war preoccupation with ensuring we had enough food and there was an emphasis on production. Joining the European Union (EU) in 1973 continued this aim through subsidies and quotas, which, with technological advances, gradually encouraged more output and higher yields via ever-larger economic units. The EU's Common Agricultural Policy seemed to fluctuate between overproducing, resulting in grain mountains and wine lakes, to underproducing, when farmers were paid to set-aside land and not produce anything. With UK farmers receiving between 50 and 75 per cent of their income from the EU's Common Agricultural Policy, life in post-Brexit rural UK was high on the list of audience questions at the festival.

With the talk over, I headed for the Jake Bugg gig, via an appointment with a pint. The bar was being very eco-friendly by encouraging customers to buy their own repeat-use Hay Festival plastic pint 'glasses'. I got a souvenir and helped to save the planet at the same time.

I can't say that I was a big Jake Bugg fan before the festival, or after it, and it was only during the performance that I realised I knew a few more of his songs than I first realised. There was a full house and a fair number of hardcore fans who sang along word-perfect with everything thrown their way. I enjoyed the gig more than I expected to be truthful and came away happy to have included it on my schedule for the trip. There was a sizeable crowd meandering back from the festival tent to the town, in a relatively light drizzle, but people hardly seemed to notice it. I got back to my yurt and snuggled down for the night in near silence, except for the gentle pitter-patter of rain on the canvas.

About half an hour later, the well-lubricated neighbours from hell turned up from their night on the town, leaving no one in any doubt about their arrival. I'm not sure to this day which yurt they were in, but I don't think it mattered. They were broadcasting to the site. It sounded like three Essex girls in a *Loose Women* type giggle-fest that was presumably fuelled by copious amounts of Prosecco. When I say girls, I imagined them to be in the forty to fifty years age range and despite sounding like lifelong pals, they didn't seem to have grasped the hang of waiting for a gap in the conversation before making their various contributions to the discussion. Apart from not having enough nerve anyway, I was reluctant to intervene. First it was mildly amusing, and second, I thought they couldn't keep it up for too long before one or more of them passed out. The volume of wine consumed worked its way through their systems, and the neighbourhood went blissfully silent for about ten minutes as the women went off in search of the toilet tent. I nearly nodded off in those ten minutes but was soon wide awake again for the last part of their broadcast. Despite being well anaesthetised, it seemed they were all feeling the cold. They gave a detailed commentary as they added more and more clothes, getting ready for bed. There was a pause, and then more uncontrolled laughter as all the remaining clothing in their luggage was also put on, piece by piece.

The ladies treated the occupants of nearby yurts to their views on various boy bands, the Spotify versus download debate, the menopause, deficiencies in partners, favourite meals and pizza toppings – which then made them all very hungry. One of the group gradually became less vocal and eventually went silent. Her battery had finally run out and to be fair to her friends, they quietened down for fear of disturbing their pal. It wasn't long before peace returned to the encampment and I could turn my attention to the hypnotic sound of rain gently drumming on the yurt. I drifted off with thoughts of the next day's ride.

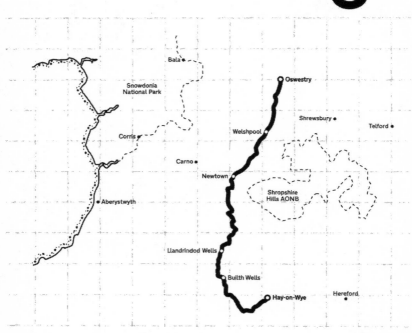

Overview Map

HAY-ON-WYE TO OSWESTRY

For anyone who doesn't know the answer to that popular pub quiz question of how much the average male bladder can hold at 2 am, I'm pleased to report that it's marginally less than a Hay Festival souvenir pint glass. That's just as well when you've booked a yurt minus en-suite facilities, and it's a long rainy trek to the camping site toilet block. Enough said.

The pleasant morning routine I'd so far established on my journey was rudely broken on day five. There was no dawn chorus, no cooked breakfast and it was lashing down with rain. This scenario wasn't quite what I had in mind when I sat at home the previous winter planning the adventure. I checked the weather forecast on my phone and it didn't look promising. Unlike yesterday's forecast, this one turned out to be 100 per cent correct. It rained for the whole of the day's ride. Rain and sheep mainly dominate my memories of that day – but that's Wales for you.

There wasn't much of a luxury camping feel about the soggy trudge down to the campsite's Portaloo toilet block at 8 am on day five. As the rain turned to a fine drizzle, thin wisps of cloud draped the trees on the surrounding hills. The scene resembled a blurred Turner landscape – one of his experimental attempts using mostly grey and a hint of green.

I wandered down for my morning bathroom duties, tooth-brush and towel in one hand and my nearly full souvenir pint glass in the other. As I approached the door to the toilet block, the only other camper around came into view and our paths converged. The guy was probably in his mid-fifties, about twenty stone, and wore a cowboy hat, grey Adidas tracksuit and blue Crocs. A life's burdens were etched onto a face that resembled a stressed Bloodhound. I guessed he must have been camping even closer to the loose women than me. I slowed down and held back to let him go ahead of me. He nodded a silent thank you. There was a pause and then we both simultaneously said, 'Mornin'. I followed up with an incredibly witty, 'Good job you've brought your sunhat'. It was the nearest I could get to witty banter in my half-awake state. He held the door for me, looked me up and down, eyed my pint glass and replied: 'Haha… are you taking the piss?' I wasn't expecting such a brilliant riposte and I'm still not sure if he meant it. Anyway, I felt well beaten in the sharp repartee stakes.

Toilet block visit over, I packed, donned my full wet weather gear again and left the yurt by about 8:30 am. At least I didn't have a key to return to the checkout. I got back to the car park, loaded up the luggage, swung my leg over the saddle and rocked the bike off its stand. The engine started first time and we chugged out of a saturated field and down to the firmer surface of the road. It was a few hundred yards from there back to the T-junction in the village of Hay-on-Wye and then left towards Builth Wells.

Riding a motorbike in the rain isn't much fun. I was warm enough. That wasn't a problem, but persistent rain is not pleasant. Although I didn't realise it, this was to be the only full day of rain on the entire trip. That's unbelievably lucky for an end to end ride through Britain and maybe some short-term compensation for the otherwise disastrous effects of climate change. I know what Kylie would have said about it… luck with the weather, I mean, not climate change.

My original plan for the day's ride was to go back to John Hillaby's walking route near Builth Wells, via a slight dogleg, then up to Ironbridge via Knighton, Clun, and Church Stretton. As my prolonged morning shower continued and I rode northward through the deluge, I went through the options for the day in my head and decided, on balance, to head home to Oswestry. I wouldn't enjoy the ride in those conditions and the forecast was for rain all day. Oswestry wasn't on John Hillaby's route, but by doubling back next morning, I could pick up his path again at Ironbridge. I'd visit the other points of interest between Hay-on-Wye and Ironbridge later in the summer, when I could easily drop down this way again on a suitable day and enjoy them properly. Right, it was decided; I'd look in at Builth Wells first, but then head up the A483 to dry out and enjoy some home comforts for the night.

I was following the course of the River Wye up to the pleasant but watery market town of Builth Wells, home to the annual Royal Welsh Show. The town lies at a point where the River Wye meets the River Irfon, but on this day, it felt more like the town was *in* the two rivers. On another day, I would have looked favourably on the town. It had a nice feel to it, several listed buildings and a magnificent 18th-century masonry bridge. The Wells part of the name was added in the 19th century to promote its spa spring water to visitors. There was no need to promote the waters on my visit; I was only too aware of copious amounts of it sluicing down.

My visit was made worthwhile, however, despite the rain, when I spotted a superb forty-foot-square mural on the end of a building. It shows the last moments of the Prince of Wales, Llywelyn ap Gruffydd, killed at the hands of the English in 1282. It's an impressive sight and quite a tourist attraction. The best bit for me is the inclusion of the blacksmith Red Madoc in the mural. According to the story, the Prince was fleeing from the English and to confuse his pursuers, the farrier reversed the shoes on the Prince's horse to make it look like he was going in the opposite direction. I don't mean to be disrespectful, but I'm afraid my mind conjured up a *Black-adder* scene with Red Madoc, aka Baldrick, implementing a very cunning plan. Like so many of those cunning plans, the reverse horseshoe trick didn't work, and the Prince sadly met his end. Sincerely though, I applaud both the concept and execution of the mural, without which I would never have known that piece of border history. I stopped to take a quick photo of the mural and headed out of town, past the permanent site of the Royal Welsh Show. There was an event going on at the showground but in those conditions I didn't feel the urge to check it out. It looked like the poor visitors were in for a soggy day. I continued up the A483 to Llandrindod Wells, onto Newport, Welshpool and finally Oswestry.

Llandrindod Wells has a certain Victorian grandeur about it and must have been quite the place to visit in its heyday. I saw a hotel advertising itself as 'the last Victorian Hydro Spa hotel in Wales', a reminder of those late 18th and 19th centuries' glory days when the town was a magnet for visitors drawn to the 'healing qualities' of the local spa waters. The town isn't far from Oswestry and I've often stopped off at one of the many cafés there as I've ridden through, knowing it's then a relatively short blast home. The water continued to pour down, but I wasn't feeling its healing qualities.

Although it wasn't a day to enjoy it, the A483 between Llandrindod Wells and Welshpool is another of those perfect twisty roads that induce a natural sway of the motorbike from side to side around gentle bends and amongst magnificent scenery.

At last, the rain eased off for a while, just as I approached a section of the A483 being upgraded to the Newtown bypass. Lorries had deposited greyish white mud all over the road as they turned in and out of the construction site. The upshot was that my view of the world gradually became more and more impressionist as tiny spots of grey spray stippled my visor. For the next four to five miles, I had a constant mist of light-coloured mud sprayed over me and just when I could have done with the torrential rain, it eased right off. I had to stop now and again to clean my visor.

I soon arrived at busy Newtown, which claims to have been a new town since the 13th century. Newtown and its neighbour Welshpool both flourished in the early 19th century on the back of the woollen industry. That was all too easy to believe on a day when all I'd seen was rain, water and sheep. Just like the tin, copper and cellophane industries, the wool industry was another that rose, flourished and then waned as other sources and cheaper alternatives became available. In its 19th-century heyday, Newtown rivalled nearby Welshpool for the glamorous title of 'international hub for the flannel industry'. The old flannel exchange, built in the early 1830s, still exists and arguably remains the grandest building in town. Present-day flannel devotees will be disappointed to read that the building is now an entertainment centre. My mind conjured up a Pythonesque vision of its former glory days with the building reverberating to the bustle of Victorian gentlemen with extravagant moustaches, black suits, silver-topped canes and top hats, brandishing facecloths from around the world. 'I bought this fine rouge specimen from a dealer in Paris and its water retention qualities are unrivalled. It has to be a contender for this year's golden tap award'… 'Oh but, my dear old thing, it's not quite a match for my prize exhibit from Argentina. This little light blue beauty is as soft as an alpaca's kiss and will have your armpits spotless in a flash'.

It wasn't small squares of material for washing your face being exchanged back in the day, of course. It was the woollen fabric associated with overalls, pyjamas or suits and in more recent times with plaid shirts. The whole Welsh border area I was riding through had been the home of the flannel industry, which also thrived in places such as Hay-on-Wye and Shrewsbury. It's possible to trace the fabric back to this area as long ago as the 16th century. Lots of rain, water and sheep were the initial winning combination but the addition of a napped finish to the woven wool (brushing the finished surface) made flannel different; this gave it a smooth and warm feel and made it very popular.

Before long I arrived in the town of Welshpool. The local rivalry with Newtown these days is more associated with their regular Welsh Premier League football fixtures. When I arrived, the rain was still pouring down and I wasn't really in the mood for sightseeing. I rode straight through and was soon out of town. As I continued up the A483, I recognised to my right the familiar outline of the three Breidden Hills and Rodney's Pillar. I knew I was getting close to Oswestry. I'd soon be with Jan, back home again. Before that, however, there were more sheep, and there was more rain.

The Welsh borders – sheep and rain

I arrived at Oswestry just after midday and found a splendid lodging for the night. It was a tidy enough place, but there were tell-tale signs that the man of the house was away, and he'd let a few jobs slip. The landlady was very accommodating, however, and a real beauty – she gave me a big kiss and a hug and said I could even share her bed for the night. I made a mental note to go back just as soon as *Another Journey through Britain* was over.

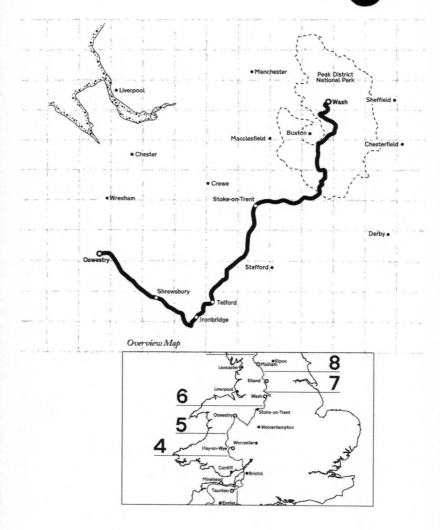

Manchester

Peak District
National Park

Liverpool

Wash

Sheffield

Macclesfield

Buxton

Chesterfield

Chester

Crewe

Wrexham

Stoke-on-Trent

Derby

Oswestry

Stafford

Shrewsbury

Telford

Ironbridge

Overview Map

Ripon
Lancaster
Malham
8

Elland
7

Liverpool

6
Wash

Oswestry
Stoke-on-Trent

5
Wolverhampton

4
Worcester

Hay-on-Wye

Cardiff
Bristol

Minehead
Taunton

Exeter

OSWESTRY TO WASH

I awoke on day six of *Another Journey through Britain* after a noisy night of thunder and lightning. By morning light, it was still rumbling around menacingly and while it was not as loud as the loose women of Hay, it was still noisy. The breakfast TV news announced that the Midlands had experienced more than a month's rainfall in one night, with several places suffering flash flooding. It delighted me to see on the weather forecast that just about every other part of the UK was basking in late spring sunshine and enjoying near-record temperatures. I was very pleased for everyone.

I did a couple of jobs on the house and mowed the lawn to pay for my accommodation. Then it was time to move on. It had been an all too brief but lovely stopover with my landlady/wife. Togged up with full wet weather gear yet again, I set off on the next leg of my adventure. With the forecast of rain all day, I knew a later departure wouldn't make any difference. I headed for Ironbridge, to pick up the trail of John Hillaby once again after my brief detour.

It's difficult to overstate the significance of the Ironbridge Gorge in terms of global history. Back in the 18th century, the area provided a fortunate coincidence of geography and geology when they discovered that iron could be made using coal instead of charcoal. The essential ingredients were conveniently found in the one-stop-shop limestone cliffs of Coalbrookdale. The Industrial Revolution was underway.

The Industrial Revolution started simultaneously in other, mainly northern, towns. But the first-ever cast-iron bridge serves to anchor the label of the 'birthplace of the Industrial Revolution' to this corner of Shropshire. Just stop and think about that late 18th-century moment in time. Think about all the industrialisation that has since taken place all around the world. And it all began there, in the English West Midlands. Steam-powered factories and mechanisation allowed Britain to become the factory of the world. There was the canal network, the coming of the railways, and colonies all around the world to keep the momentum going. It was massive and elevated Britain to the position of a dominant world power for years to follow. And that iconic bridge constructed in 1781, over the River Severn, is still there.

Ironbridge rightly deserves to be a UNESCO World Heritage Site, but on my visit, the bridge itself wasn't looking such a grand sight. It was cocooned in plastic sheeting while it underwent a £3.6 million restoration. A bit of a facelift after 250 years seems fair enough, but it was terrible timing on my part. Ironbridge would have to be another place for a follow-up visit. At least this one was relatively close to home.

The rain had thankfully eased off and I had a brief wander around the town. I hadn't realised until my visit that the town was also famous for being the home of Britain's last remaining teddy bear factory. I looked around the Ironbridge visitor centre and had a chat with the staff. Here I came across those very typical, slightly melodic, West Midlands accents. Everyone sounded, to my ear, like either Julie Walters or Ozzie Osbourne. There were lots of rounded Brummie vowels and 'Did I know that Ironbridge was one of the ten most-visited UNESCO World Heritage Sites in Britain with over five hundred thousand visitors per year?' I wandered out for a last look at the plastic covered bridge before moving on. It was a pity to see just a Lego-like version of the iconic bridge rather than the naked genuine thing. But on the bright side, it had stopped raining.

I soon settled back into the rhythm of the ride. It was good to see that the weather, and for a large part, the road, had at last dried up again. Some clown coming the other way in a Ford Focus suddenly made me jump out of my skin. He was flashing his car's headlights like some drug-crazed rave DJ as I cruised along nonchalantly towards Staffordshire. Bloody idiot. I was still recovering my composure and wondering what all the fuss was about when I rounded the next bend to find the whole of the left side of the road covered in floodwater. Fortunately, I was going slowly enough to have stopped if I needed to, but I could dodge around the floodwater on the other, mercifully empty, side of the road. It was a timely reminder that it's impossible to switch off for a moment on a motorcycle – you need to be concentrating every second. It also reminded me that drivers coming the other way flashing their lights might not be drug-crazed DJs.

Norbury Junction on the Shropshire Union Canal

I rode on to Norbury Junction, a key point on the Shropshire Union Canal and site of the Junction Inn, used by John Hillaby on his way towards Stoke. I get the impression he made the most of the old canal and disused railway networks to enjoy an easy-going ramble on the gentle gradients. Why wouldn't you? I parked up for half an hour to stretch my legs, visit the Junction Inn and have a cheeky ice cream now that the clouds were thinning out – things were looking up again.

Next stop on the day's ride was Stoke-on-Trent and believe it or not, there were clear blue skies over the city as I approached. Stoke and blue skies are not a combination of words I'd normally expect to see together. As a born and bred southerner, my definition of 'grim up north' starts somewhere around Stoke – for no logical reason and with no real justification, but regional stereotypes are like that. I feel I can say this now because having moved to Shropshire, I'm a borderline northerner myself. Oswestry is maybe more north Midlands, I guess, but working out regional boundaries is debatable and highly subjective. Talking of which, I have come across at least three plausible theories for the location of the British north-south dividing line. The three approaches have varying degrees of academic legitimacy ranging from some to none. If you're interested, and who wouldn't be, you'll probably need a good GB atlas to follow this next bit.

Let's start with the most obvious north-south dividing line, which, for reasons that will become apparent, I will call the Roman theory. This one is the most obvious because it is real and visible to this day with the naked eye. The Romans built Hadrian's Wall where they did for an excellent reason. The Roman emperor Hadrian came to Britain in the year AD 122 and decided that a seventy-five-mile wall was necessary from the west to east coasts to mark the northern edge of the Roman Empire. That formidable barrier would keep the Romans, let's say the southerners, safe from the barbarians – let's call them the northerners. For a while, his successor, Emperor Antoninus Pius, must have thought northerners were not so bad after all; maybe the actual threat was further up country. The Romans then built the Antonine Wall across the central belt of Scotland. It only lasted for about twenty years, at which point they retreated to Hadrian's Wall. Maybe the earlier definition of where the barbarian lands began had been correct after all. The wall runs from the Solway Firth in the west to the River Tyne in the east. In doing so, it crosses Britain on a line that includes to its south much of what we think of today as northern England.

The second theory I've come across suggests a more diagonal north-south dividing line that follows the path of Watling Street, which is roughly the line of the modern-day A2 and A5 roads. I'll call this one the Watling Street theory. This ancient trackway, which pre-dates the Roman occupation, ran from Canterbury in the south, via a ford over the Thames at Westminster, up to St Alban's and then north-westwards as far as Wroxeter, near Shrewsbury in Shropshire. When the Romans arrived, they loved the route, immediately saw the military and economic benefits and upgraded it to a proper paved Roman road. They also linked it to several English Channel ports. Their Watling Street Roman road would have been the M1 superhighway of its day, but hopefully with better service areas. The next foreign invaders, the Vikings, began their excursions to Britain around AD 800 and stayed, on and off, for just over 200 years. A map of late 9th century England would show Watling Street as effectively the front line. The road was the dividing line between the Viking influenced north and east, under Danelaw and the Anglo-Saxon regions of Mercia and Wessex to the south and west. With fortifications along the line to re-enforce the division, this became a north-south cultural dividing line, or so the theory goes. That alignment is entirely at odds with the Hadrian's Wall version, however. It also suggests that large swathes of East Anglia and some Home Counties fall into the 'north' category – I don't think so.

Which brings me to the third, and my preferred, definition of the north-south divide. I call this one the Doric theory, named after the pub in Waterloo, Liverpool, where this significant cultural discovery first came to light. My other working title was 'the spontaneous urinal dialogue theory', but I don't think that's so snappy as the shorter version. This evidence-based theory stems from the mid-1970s when I left my Southampton home as a soft southern teenager. My first two postings as an OS surveyor were to Birmingham and Liverpool. Culture shock doesn't come near to describing the experience and I considered myself lucky to have emerged from both cities largely unscathed.

Imagine the horror of this scene…

I was standing in the gents' toilet of the Doric pub late one evening, doing what was colloquially known at the time as 'pointing Percy at the porcelain'. A stereotypical 1970s Scouser (complete with perm, 'tache and shell suit – I kid you not) was standing next to me and, out of the blue, engaged me in conversation. He said something like (try the Scouse accent yourself) 'Aaright mate, gorra ciggy?' What was he thinking? Was he off his face with cheap northern ale? I'd never met the guy in my life, I had no subtitles to go on, and there he was just talking to me, a complete stranger. I soon discovered that the behaviour wasn't a one-off. Up north, they seemed to do that sort of thing all the time – they'd talk to complete strangers! The practice wasn't confined to gents' toilets, but this was where I first came across the disturbing phenomenon. Standing at the urinal is usually a place where one keeps oneself to oneself, so the shocking experience became etched on my memory.

As I moved around Britain with my work, I kept a mental note of where this disconcerting practice took place. With a cartographer's aptitude for spatial awareness, I gradually built up a map in my mind of where the north-south divide ran. Based upon the Doric theory, I reckoned it was a line between Chester (not so far from Wroxeter of theory two) and Grimsby. I could comment on the Grim in Grimsby, but I will resist. So, there you have it: three theories and three different definitions of where to draw the north-south dividing line. Anthropologists have no doubt been locked in this debate for decades. In the case of northern anthropologists, that might even be while standing next to each other at the urinals.

I was still less than halfway into *Another Journey through Britain*. As I rode up through the West Country, along the Welsh Borders and across the Midlands, I was trying to keep my ear tuned to the regional accents and dialects – trying to detect changes as I travelled northwards. I was comparing what I heard with the descriptions given by John Hillaby, fifty years ago. My conclusion, at that point, was that the boundaries had changed little. They have remained remarkably geographically stable over the years despite the changes in demographics, the wider dispersion of families and the general increase in population movement around the country. Likewise, I saw little change in the north-south dividing line either, at least not if based on the most plausible of the three definitions – the Doric theory.

As I approached the outskirts of Stoke, I came to a fork in the road. The signpost gave directions to Stoke City's Britannia Stadium one way and to Alton Towers the other way. Thrill-seekers would have no difficulty in choosing which way to go, although Stoke City supporters might argue they had been on their own vertical drop roller-coaster ride the previous season. I cruised around Stoke city centre twice, trying to follow the signs for the Potteries Museum. After two unproductive circuits, I decided I wouldn't have enough fuel, or daylight, to see that one through to a conclusion and gave up. I chose instead to follow the signs for the Moorcroft factory. At least those signs led to the intended destination, but I found it shut when I arrived – ah yes, it was Bank Holiday Sunday.

Stoke city centre was grim. I find it hard to think of any redeeming features. My lasting impression is of rows of boarded-up shops. Among the ones not boarded up, there was a high proportion of betting offices, vape stores and kebab shops. More serious evidence than my fleeting impression backs up this sweeping generalisation. A report in 2017 described how over 30 per cent of the shops in the Stoke-on-Trent town of Burslem were left vacant. Sadly, you can see this same situation in town centres across Britain. I read that Britain has twice as many shops as it needs – at a time when there's insufficient housing to go around.

The chilly wind of change blowing the metaphorical tumbleweed past the boarded-up shopfronts of our town's high streets is a sad feature of travelling through Britain. It's an unwelcome turn for the worse since John Hillaby's walk in 1966, made even worse when the Covid-19 pandemic arrived. It isn't just the retail sector that has borne the brunt. Bank branches have closed at a rate of 1,000 per year over recent years, driven by the need to cut costs as more people do their banking online. You can see the same trend with restaurants and pubs, the latter having declined in numbers by over 25 per cent since 1966 and sometimes the figure feels higher. Increasingly, people stay at home and drink cheap supermarket booze while they play their video games, stream online films and, if they want to, smoke.

The reasons behind the demise of Britain's town centres are many. The collapse of traditional local industries such as mining, steel, shipbuilding, or with Stoke, the Potteries, is a significant factor. Throw in the impact of online shopping, inflexible business rates and unhelpful car parking policies (and then a pandemic) and you have a perfect storm. Some towns are fighting back, and these must surely be the templates for others to follow, if the circumstances allow. Altrincham, for example, was once labelled a ghost town. It came back to life, before Covid-19 struck, by developing a revival plan that included council cash for business loans, training, improved public transport, revamped shopfronts and the revival of the traditional market area. The result was a flourishing of independent shops and the metamorphosis of the town centre into a social meeting place. The number of vacant shops fell and the numbers of people visiting rose steadily… so it *can* be done, although I don't doubt it is difficult in many towns with less favourable starting points.

On one of my forlorn circuits of the city's inner ring-road looking for the Potteries Museum, I saw signs to the 'Cultural Quarter'. The thought of a cultural quarter in Stoke induced an involuntary chuckle but made me realise that things couldn't be as bad as my first impressions. But those had been depressing. To provide a balanced view, Stoke-on-Trent is another name that deserves its place in the annals of Britain's industrial heritage. Names like the Etruria Works, Wedgwood, Moorcroft and Spode are renowned the world over. I guessed the Potteries Museum must have been in the Cultural Quarter, but I hadn't managed to find it.

As I made my way out of the city centre towards the Peak District, I was lucky to avoid being totally enveloped by several giant potholes in the roads. Highway engineers of Stoke, please note. I continued to motor north-east, my previous unfounded indictment of the city at least now having some evidence to back it up.

For additional balanced comment, I should add that John Hillaby liked Stoke. He found a barber's shop, plenty to eat, and friendly people. He stopped off at a launderette, where he watched a young girl removing a man's shirt and underwear from one of the machines. He noticed the girl wasn't wearing a wedding ring! His observation alludes to the moral attitudes of the time. I don't think anyone nowadays would notice or comment on such a thing. Views on marriage have changed enormously in the last fifty years and the 1960s' pattern of courting, engagement, marriage and then having children seems distinctly old-fashioned in today's world. Statistics can mislead, but the figures for marriage and divorce show a clear trend. In non-precise, rounded statistics, the number of weddings per year in Britain has gone down to around 60 per cent of the 1966 figure, while the number of divorces has more than doubled. That the Office of National

Statistics nowadays counts the number of 'same-sex marriages' is another comment on social change. There is no longer any social stigma attached to couples living together 'out of wedlock' or children being born to non-wedded couples. Even the concept of gender and what constitutes couples has become blurred. As a husband of forty years, with three children all born after our wedding day, I feel a bit of a freak these days. Anyway, back to John Hillaby and his experience of the Potteries. He wrote affectionately that it was easily the dirtiest place he visited, but also the friendliest.

I stopped briefly at Cauldon Lowe, another place on John Hillaby's route and also the site of a vast limestone quarry he described as the biggest in the world. The quarry is still there and also a cement works, but the place was closed when I arrived and with CCTV cameras much in evidence, I didn't want to go poking around too much.

The Peak District

As I headed towards Buxton, the countryside transformed. I was now back in upland moorland scenery for the first time since Exmoor, but here the rocks were red and brown mill-stone. They were gritty – like northerners (I consider that a positive trait, of course, now that I'm living in the north myself). I had ridden from Ironbridge in Shropshire to Buxton in Derbyshire and as I transited from the West to East Midlands, I reckoned I must have been bumping along the edge of that south-north divide as defined by the Doric theory. From here until the Scottish Borders I would be int' north.

I was at last in the Peak District National Park, part of the country I'd not explored much over the years. I rode through Buxton and into the little hamlet of Wash, near Chapel-en-le-Frith. The plan was to meet up with my nephew, Mark, who rode down from his home in Elland, near Halifax. He would join me for the evening and tomorrow's ride. Somehow the plan worked, and he arrived five minutes after me at our guesthouse accommodation for the night. We unpacked our things into our rooms, and our lovely host, Diane, made us welcome. As soon as she discovered my background, she whipped out an attractive OS Tourist map of the Peak District. Refreshed with afternoon tea and cakes and with a map to look at, I was very content. The weather had behaved itself for the second half of the day and evening sunshine greeted us as we left the cottage in search of dinner and copious northern beverages.

Accompanied by Bob the Labrador, Diane guided Mark and me along the local footpaths and showed us the shortcut to Chapel-en-le-Frith. There we spent a most enjoyable evening eating local fare (well, northern pizzas), drinking northern beers and planning our ride for the next day.

Listening tut accents at t' bar there were no doubt I were definitely up north. There was a relatively broad cross-section of drinkers at the Kings Arms that evening. The majority were heavily tattooed young men in shorts with closely cropped hair; an 'undercut' is the correct term for it, I think. Had I not been such a cool biker dude, I might have felt out of place in that company. The place was buzzing and there was a boisterous but friendly, i.e. northern, feel to the place.

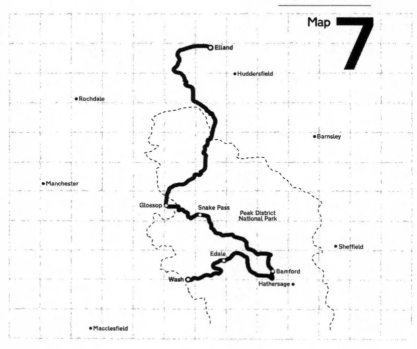

Map

7

- Elland
- Huddersfield
- Rochdale
- Barnsley
- Manchester
- Glossop
- Snake Pass
- Peak District National Park
- Edale
- Sheffield
- Bamford
- Wash
- Hathersage
- Macclesfield

Overview Map

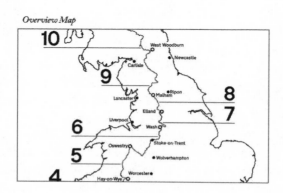

- 10
- West Woodburn
- Newcastle
- Carlisle
- 9
- Lancaster
- Malham
- Ripon
- 8
- Elland
- Liverpool
- Wash
- 7
- 6
- Oswestry
- Stoke-on-Trent
- 5
- Wolverhampton
- 4
- Worcester
- Hay-on-Wye

WASH TO ELLAND

First things first: I need to make an apology. I'm so sorry, Peak District. I never realised how incredible you are; why haven't I been visiting you for years?!

Mark 1 and Mark 2 both surfaced by 9 am on day seven of *Another Journey through Britain*. We enjoyed a light breakfast and were soon poring over the Peak District map again to choose the best route for the day. The day had started with glorious sunshine and the forecast was for the weather to remain good. After our deliberations of the previous night and with local knowledge supplied by our host, Diane, we soon worked our way through the alphabet to arrive at plan Z. Nephew Mark mentioned in passing that his Honley 125cc motorcycle could do with a drop of chain lube. Diane was on to it in a flash, dashing out of the house and returning with friendly neighbour Paul before you could say dusty links. Paul was from the Type 1 school of vehicle maintenance – the one where they have to do stuff even when it's not needed. To our great appreciation, Paul soon had both bikes sorted out with superbly lubricated chains and we were ready. People can be so generous and kind and, in my experience, you meet so many of those people when you're on an adventure.

As part of my research before the road trip, I'd discovered that there were two underground show caves in the Peak District, called Peak and Speedwell Caverns. Our overnight accommodation was near to both of them. Peak Cavern goes under the alternative title of 'The Devil's Arse' and visiting Speedwell involves an underground boat trip. I found myself more drawn to the latter. Nephew Mark was happy to go along with the idea, so after we'd downed our coffees and packed our things, we set off to ride the four miles to the caves.

As we left the B&B, there was a lovely fresh feel to the morning air, before it had been warmed up to full working temperature for the day. The Derbyshire lanes reminded me of Devon at first. They were narrow, twisty and wooded, but before long they morphed into the more characteristic Peak District landscape of open moorland and big skies. Speedwell Cavern is about halfway down the Winnats Pass, where the winding road reaches over 20 per cent gradient in places, in a narrow limestone gorge to the west of Castleton. We soon found the car park for the cavern and immediately opposite, the ticket office, gift shop and entrance to the cave system.

The tunnels we were going to visit resulted from 18th-century lead mining activities. The old mining tunnels are part of a vast underground labyrinth that spreads for miles; they link up with natural caves and caverns that have formed over millennia in the Carboniferous rocks under the hills of the Peak District.

The Peak District lies between Sheffield, Manchester, Stoke and Nottingham. The short distance and ease of access from those large centres of population explain why this National Park is Britain's most popular. There are 13.25 million visitors per year according to official statistics and it felt like most of them had turned up on the day Mark and I visited. Being on motorbikes, however, we could cruise past the queuing traffic and into the car park of Speedwell Cavern, with barely disguised smugness. Not only did we find space for our bikes, but we could park for free. As we walked over the road to the cave entrance, we again passed lengthy lines of cars stretched out in both directions, in near gridlock. Their exasperated owners took it in turns to enter the car park, complete a circuit, realise there was nowhere to park and then try to exit, past the cars still waiting to get in.

Our smugness soon evaporated when we saw the line of people queuing for the ticket office. Nephew Mark was too polite to say what I knew he must be thinking. First, who in their right mind would choose a sunny Bank Holiday to visit a major tourist attraction like this, when the world and his wife would also be there? Second, given such a glorious sunny day, why would you then want to spend your precious leisure time underground in the dark?

We were committed to the mission by then, so we were going to see it through. The other people in the queue seemed patient and good-natured and the hour waiting to get to the ticket office and into the cave seemed to pass quickly. Some people even spoke to complete strangers in the queue, confirming our position relative to the famous Chester/Grimsby line. Local fudge and the old favourite queuing game of guess the colour of the next motorbike to go past mitigated the monotony of the wait. We played the traditional rules whereby only bikes travelling up the road counted. I lost the first round on a technicality; I guessed the wrong colour. It was necessary to persuade nephew Mark to go for best of three – and then five. I can't remember who won.

With mounting excitement, we finally reached the ticket office. The camaraderie of the queue, built up over sixty minutes of shared adversity, erupted into mutual congratulations and relief. There were smiles all round for making it through to the ticket office on a Bank Holiday; we'd made it to the caves!

Twenty-one people at a time were allowed to pass through the turnstile. As our group edged towards the caves, we were instructed to don blue safety helmets. We were briefed, briefly, and in we went. The temperature plummeted as our guide led us through cold, dripping, but well-lit tunnels that echoed the group's nervous excitement. Our guide took us down 106 wet and uneven limestone steps to a waiting boat which by a stroke of luck could carry twenty-one people. The long metal boat bobbed about in a flooded tunnel and clanged against the landing stage as we boarded one by one. When the boat was fully loaded and balanced, our brave crew was given a few more words of reassurance and we gently pulled away down the tunnel into the darkness. Initially, we glided along in total silence.

The voyage didn't feel at all dangerous but might not be ideal for the claustrophobic; there were only a few feet of tunnel to spare either side of the boat and above our heads. The safety hats weren't just to make us look good. Our vessel cruised smoothly forward down the former lead mine adit, propelled by an electric motor. Our guide's voice echoed around anonymously in the dark as he told us the story of the mine.

Apart from the light on the front of the boat, all around us was cold and drippy darkness. The tunnel was only wide enough for one boat but about 200 metres into our voyage we came across a wider section that formed a passing place. We loitered in this underground lay-by for a few minutes and saw the bow-light of another boat coming the other way. It was soon alongside. A brief outburst of lively banter between the two crews ensued, which echoed around the tunnel and then gradually faded as we progressed on our separate courses. While the other boat headed back to the stairway and exit, we travelled a further 200 metres into the adit.

As we continued our cruise, the guide entertained us with facts and figures about the formation of the caves and the search for lead back in the late 1700s. He interlaced these matter-of-fact statistics with an inexhaustible supply of cave-related jokes. Most of them were so groaningly bad they were good. This was a gift of a job for someone with tunnel vision, dark humour, and a mine of historical information. You get the picture. Between cave-related gags we were told that the mine had cost its original owners around £14,000 but had only ever yielded about £3,000 worth of lead. According to our guide, this had gone down like a lead balloon – and so it went on.

Mark and I rushed through some dubious back-of-a-fag-packet calculations and estimated that the boat trips were probably making a few thousand pounds per day so we couldn't help but question the original business model back in the 18th century – they should've just dug tunnels and taken people around in boats from the outset.

At the furthest point of the journey, we all disembarked inside an impressive limestone cavern and had a few minutes to take photos. It had been worth the journey to get there, and the rock formations were dramatic, but the possibility to explore any further was limited and it was soon time to return to the surface. We boarded the boat once again and made the reverse trip back to the landing stage and the 106 wet and uneven limestone steps. When we got to the passing place again, our guide egged us on to scare the new visitors with tales of cave monsters and missing tourists… he had to keep it interesting.

Mark and I emerged blinking into the bright sunlight like two prisoners caught in a searchlight, surfacing from an escape tunnel into the night. My internal jukebox changed the background music from Going Underground to Band on the Run. When we'd readjusted to the light enough not to bump into anyone, we re-stocked with fudge and made our way back to the car park and our bikes. Once again, we took plea-sure in gliding nonchalantly past the grid-locked motorists. We cruised past them and headed for Edale – the start of the Pennine Way.

Although the South-West Coast Path (630 miles) is longer, the Pennine Way is considered the ultimate test for long-distance walkers in Britain. It runs 268 miles up the Pennine spine of the country from Edale to Kirk Yetholm on the Scottish Borders. Its reputation, particularly in the early stages, suggests a boot ensnaring muddy trek across windswept uplands. John Hillaby wasn't a big fan of the start of the trail; he described it as being extraordinarily depressing. The walk must have been miserable for him, with the clouds down and the rain driving in horizontally, but on a pleasant day the moors look magnificent.

It was time for lunch, so we tucked in at the Rambler Inn, in Edale. We lazed around in the sunshine for an hour or so in the beer garden. The place was heaving with bikers, walkers and just about every other type of tourist imaginable. When OS analysed the 800,000 routes being created and shared on its walking App in 2019, the favourite place in Great Britain for starting a walk turned out to be Edale. No surprise there. The Peak District takes the top two positions on the list, with Fairholmes, in the Derwent Valley grabbing second spot.

When John Hillaby passed through Edale fifty years earlier, he mentions that the village was swarming with visitors of all descriptions, including a category he described as 'indolent'. I made a mental note to add that under-used word to my vocabulary – it means 'showing an inclination to avoid exertion'. He observed that as the walkers were heading for the hills, the indolent were meandering around looking for somewhere to make love.

Crikey, what sort of trip was he on? It was the swinging sixties, I guess, and just a year before the Summer of Love. I could see no sign of people making love in the beer garden of the Ramblers Inn, but I guess lazily mooching our way to the pub for a lunchtime picnic had put us bikers in the 'indolents' category.

In his *Journey through Britain* book, John Hillaby was fulsome in his praise for Tom Stephenson, the man credited with devising the Pennine Way route during the 1930s. The final section was officially opened in 1965, a year before John Hillaby arrived in Edale as part of his great walk. Most of the moors are privately owned and prior to the opening of the Pennine Way, access had been denied to the public. Tom Stephenson's dream was for a 'Long Green Trail – from the Peak to the Cheviots' and accessible to the public in the same way that the Appalachian Trail had become in the USA since the 1930s.

John Hillaby was less effusive in his praise for the Ramblers' Association pamphlet he used to follow the route along the Pennine Way. Let's be generous and assume it was the early days, that some parts of the path were still being defined, and the leaflet was still a work in progress. It must have been early days because he also relates how he only saw seven or eight walkers in the eleven days that it took him to walk to the Scottish border. Around 2,000 walkers complete the length of the long-distance path each year nowadays, and hundreds of thousands more enjoy shorter stretches of it.

I read the *Journey through Britain* extract about Edale to nephew Mark while we lazed indolently in the beer garden. The day was warm; the sun was high. It tempted me to wear some flowers in my hair and feel a strange vibration, all across the nation – but I was fifty years too late. Just as well, because nephew Mark wouldn't have had a clue what was happening and would probably have been quite disturbed by the sight.

We saddled up once again and headed out of Edale. I was still mentally in my tie-dye and flares as we headed down the beautiful River Noe valley towards Brough. I got the Summer of Love out of my system with a medley of songs – adapting the words for the occasion. The old Scott McKenzie favourite, for example, became 'If you're goin' to visit Edale, be sure to put… some oil on your chain'.

I just hope Daniel Craig's voice is up to this when they make the film version of this book. Most of these oldie references will mean absolutely nothing to many people, so I'll move swiftly on. Luckily for nephew Mark, my 'musical' efforts were well smothered by the loud rumble of a Royal Enfield.

Our Peak District Bank Holiday visit coincided with the annual sheepdog trials in Bamford, about twelve miles from Edale. By a masterstroke of strategic planning, the next highlight of the day was that very sheepdog trial. I don't mind admitting that as we approached the village, I was anxious about how the verdict would go.

Bamford sheep dog trials

Bamford lies in the heart of the Peak District and is surrounded by high moorland. Its history can be traced back to the Domesday Book, but in modern times it provides a convenient base for tourists who go there for walking, cycling and fishing. One of the interesting features of the village is the Anglers Rest, which in recent years has become a village community pub. All along my route, I was seeing the impact on towns and villages of disappearing pubs. I was observing first hand how so many were being lost. The ones surviving frequently seemed to have diversified, but in doing so, some were losing their traditional role as the social gathering place for the community.

At the time that John Hillaby came through the Peak District, there were several pubs in Bamford, but one by one they closed until the Anglers Rest was the only one left. When the owners called last orders for what seemed to be the final time, the local community rallied round to save the day. The village post office was also under threat, so 340 villagers collectively raised £275,000 and became shareholders in a community group to save the pub and the post office. Their hard work paid off and in 2013 resulted in a viable village pub, a relocated post office, and a colourful café, all served by a large village car park. It saved the pub; the village kept its community focus, and it provided significant local employment.

According to the Campaign for Real Ale (CAMRA), eighteen pubs were closing per week in Britain in early 2019, almost a thousand a year, but the community pub idea seems to be spreading. There are now over fifty across Britain, with plenty more community groups actively working to set up others. I'll raise a glass to that – cheers!

The two Marks arrived in Bamford by early afternoon, and we soon found the field where the sheepdog trials were taking place. A very amiable man on the gate let us in for free – because we were bikers, and I had a classic old motorcycle. Again, I've just made that bit up for added interest if the kind man will get into trouble. I didn't have the heart (and was too stingy) to shatter his illusion by telling him that my bike was only a year old. It was a lovely friendly gesture and gratefully accepted.

We parked up and made our way through to the huge field where the principal event was taking place. Our first impressions were of a typical English country fair. The first section of the field was flat and contained one large marquee and many smaller ones. There was an assortment of agricultural produce for sale and lots of farm-related stuff going on.

Two rows of chairs were lined up behind a rope that crossed the lush green field and on the other side of the rope, the sheepdog trials were already underway. That part of the field disappeared away into the distance. The rolling Derbyshire fells formed a very picturesque backdrop, and the entire scene was quintessentially rural England. Unfortunately, we arrived too late to take part in the annual fell race, so we had to content ourselves instead with an ice cream and an hour watching the sheepdogs under cross-examination.

Mark and I observed, open-mouthed in bewilderment, as a series of shepherds took turns to impress the judges. We were both new to the sheepdog trial scene, but we gradually picked up the way it worked. A shepherd walked out from the main marquee into the large field, with two dogs. There were no sheep anywhere in sight at this point, just two white sheep pens – the kind you see on the TV programme *One Man and His Dog*. The shepherd then whistled, and the dogs flew off into the distance: one off to the left and the other to the right. They were ridiculously rapid as they sped off and then became just a blur as they made the jump to light speed. And I mean really into the distance – so far that they disappeared from view. It looked for all the world as though they had just done a runner and would never be seen again. Ha, not much of a trial. A few more whistles and then tiny dots appeared on the horizon. It turned out to be a group of four sheep being steered towards us by the two dogs. The sheep gradually became clearer and larger as they were brought across the huge field towards the line of spectators. The dogs could also be seen again, still in blurred form as they dashed one way and then the next. The shepherd continued to whistle, occasionally breaking off to bellow something loud and staccato in Derbyshire agri-speak. Mark and I eventually realised that the four sheep were heading our way between two marker poles. On the shepherd's whistle or shouted command, the dogs would in turns collapse to the ground as if shot, leap up again and fly off, and then collapse down again. It was fascinating to watch. After rounding the marker poles, the dogs steered the sheep towards and into one of the white pens. The achievement resulted in wildly enthusiastic applause from an appreciative audience.

It was all very impressive and took place in front of a sizeable and seemingly knowledgeable crowd. I tried to tune in and pick up the comments of the surrounding people, but we seemed to be amongst foreigners… 'Ooh heck, look art, eez come by too early therr'. Lots of the spectators had their own dogs and I was impressed by how all the spectator dogs somehow knew that it wasn't their job to sort the sheep out; they were just there to observe. Each shepherd must sound different to their own dogs, I guess, and just as well. I imagined a scene in which a shepherd whistled and suddenly all the watching dogs dashed off, and all turned left and right in unison at the various commands, like a murmuration of border collies. Some of them looked up for it.

I could have stayed longer. I found it strangely mesmerising and I appreciated the skills of the shepherds. There is always something to be admired when watching an expert who is completely at the top of their sport or profession. I sensed this wasn't the high adrenalin excitement to hold the attention of a twenty-four-year-old biker, however, so I suggested we move on. I knew nephew Mark had been looking forward all day to riding over the Snake Pass, so I didn't want to hold him up too long.

We rode down the A6013 and picked up the A57 Snake Road at Ladybower Reservoir. My research had told me that the stretch of road from Ladybower Reservoir to Glossop over the Snake Pass is another of those classic biker routes. My *Bikers' Britain* guidebook suggested it might be the most scenic ride in the Peak District – and we weren't disappointed.

The road was another lovely 'twisty', curving one way and then the next through classic moorland scenery. There were one or two sharp bends and blind summits, so the road had to be taken seriously, but at the geriatric pace I'm used to travelling at, it was a great pleasure. I stopped on the crest of the pass to take some photos. It was a spot where you could see for miles over barren moors and where *Simpsons*-type puffy white clouds tried their best to fill impossibly big skies. Mark pulled up next to me in a lay-by and we realised that we'd somehow picked the spot where the Pennine Way crossed the main road. The long-distance path looked hard work at that point, even on a perfect summer's day. I would hate to see it on a day when the cloud was down and the rain was blowing horizontally. We'd taken a considerably shorter route than the twelve-mile trail from Edale that John Hillaby had taken over the blanket bog of Kinder Scout. We seemed to be having a much better day than he had, when he passed this way.

Mark and I were having so much fun we did it all again. We went back down to the reservoir and then rode back up – taking it in turns to capture some photos. Looking back, it was a nice relaxing way to spend some time. It felt good to slow down for a change, rather than worrying about making progress and ticking off more miles.

When we'd got that out of our system, we carried on down the Snake Road to Glossop. Once again it was a delightful series of bends, where you could lean one way then the other – more twists than a Chubby Checker top ten hit… to show my age again. We then headed south and back to our previous night's accommodation in the village of Wash, completing a most enjoyable circular tour of the southern Peak District.

There was plenty more to discover another time. We collected the luggage that our host, Diane, had kindly let us leave with her for the day and had a relaxing cup of tea while we went through the highlights of our day.

Tea and gossip done, the two Marks headed out again and rode north to the next night's stopover in Elland. I was going to stay with my sister-in-law, Lesley, and her husband,

Arthur. As we rode northwards, I reflected on another eventful day. We had clattered around in a metal boat in the Speedwell Caves, had lunch in Edale, watched the sheepdogs of Derbyshire and sampled the beauty of the Snake Pass road. I was already looking forward to the next day, – one of my favourite parts of the country – the Yorkshire Dales!

Map

8

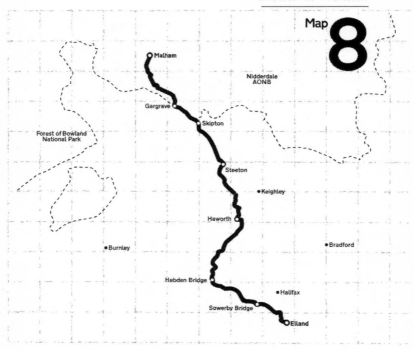

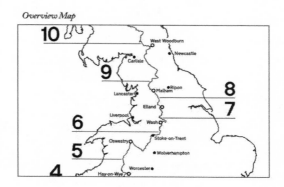

Overview Map

ELLAND TO MALHAM

'A disagreeable story'.
'Wild, confused, disjointed, and improbable'.
'A compound of vulgar depravity'.
'The only consolation... is that it will never be read'.
'A pile of crap'.

These quotes aren't publishers' feedback on the draft manuscript of my book; they are comments from critics of the day (in 1847) when *Wuthering Heights* was published. Alright, I added the last one myself, but I'm confident it reflects the critical consensus of the time.

The Parsonage at Haworth, where the Brontës lived, was on my list of places to visit on day eight of my adventure and was a brief ride away from my starting point in Elland. *Wuthering Heights* is one of the greatest literary classics ever written, which makes it hard to imagine how it could have been a flop at the time of its publication. Keeping in mind how wrong the literary critics can be is a straw that I cling to.

I had spent a most enjoyable Monday night with my relatives. It was a treat to have such a comfortable night with marvellous company and to at last tango in Halifax. Lesley took me out for a proper Yorkshire breakfast first thing in the morning and then packed me on my way with an emergency Yorkshire pork pie for later. With the bike loaded up, I rode off into grey and blustery conditions. It was dry, which I'll always take, but not quite the blue skies of the previous day. My meandering route for the day was to take me west at first and then north, towards Sowerby (pronounced by the locals as Sore-bee), onto Mytholmroyd (Mithem-royd) and then up to Hebden Bridge (Hebden Bridge). I'd then continue north- wards to Haworth and then stop overnight at Malham. The thought of being back in the Yorkshire Dales again that evening was exciting, but I was also curious about what lay between me and my ultimate destination that day. What oddi- ties would the day throw up this time? Or would it just be a regulation ride with nothing happening? I doubted it.

Leaving Elland, I rode for some time down a long road bordered by an equally long stone wall. The road sign on the wall read, 'LONG WALL'. Now I'm sure there are people out there who might find that helpful, but if you ask me, that's just overkill. The council would be better off spending their brass on emptying t' bins.

I cruised through nondescript grey urban-ness. When I look back to my notes for this section of the journey... well, there aren't any. I think I was just getting through the area in a mixture of mild curiosity and resignation; I was looking forward to the next highlights on my list of places to visit. I remember feeling that my morning ride warranted a back- ground commentary in the form of a depressed Alan Bennett monologue. As if recognising a potential slide into melan- choly, the jukebox in my head came up with a Yorkshire covers playlist to raise my mood. A downbeat, 'Nowt compares t' thee', from Sinead O'Connor was amusing but not exactly uplifting. The Three Degrees contributed a more upbeat 'When will I sithee again', and Dire Straits rounded the session off with a rousing rendition of 'Brass for Nowt'.

In my sixty-plus years, I've lived in many parts of Britain. Starting in Hampshire, I moved to Kent, then the New Forest,

Southampton, Birmingham, Liverpool, Shropshire, Leicester-shire, Ayrshire, Cornwall, Southampton again, the Scottish Highlands and back to Shropshire. I've also lived in France and worked for the last thirty years all around the world. I don't mention this to fabricate a reputation as an enigmatic international man of mystery, but more to explain that I have become accustomed to adapting to unfamiliar places. I feel comfortable in unusual surroundings – but *not* around the West Yorkshire and Lancashire parts of northern of England. That's so weird. I can only surmise that a wicked mill owner must have beaten me mercilessly in a previous life. At least that's the most logical explanation.

Those West Yorkshire urban districts have a peculiar fascination, however. I felt I was riding through a famous chapter of British history. It was quite a smoke-filled, borderline satanic mills chapter, but this former industrial landscape was once the workshop of the world. Whatever misgivings I might have had, I felt a tangible sense of its historical significance. This is where the Industrial Revolution unfolded.

The urban geography of the area is unlike anywhere else I know in Britain. Polycentric pockets of smoke-stained old mill towns give way to wild and open expanses of moor-land... then you are plunged back into the next little island of industrial Lowry-scape. One thing I like about this area is how so many of the old textile mills have survived, even if many of them are now deluxe apartments or business units. Some of them are imposing in their grandeur – massive rectangular blocks of brick and glass – with a chimney. They are the magnificent and beautiful plus-size models of the old factory world. Just to see them still standing loud and proud is a nostalgic reminder of the heyday of the Industrial Revolution. Coalbrookdale in Shropshire might have had the first iron bridge, but this part of West Yorkshire and neighbouring Lancashire to the west were the real engine houses of the revolution. By the end of the 1700s, textile mills were churning out clothing on an unprecedented scale. Large-scale manufacturing had kicked off for the first time in history – anywhere. It made minor fortunes for the mill owners. Canals, turnpike roads and then railways transported the end products to the growing cities and then further afield. Squint your eyes in some places and you can still see that smoke-filled 19th-century industrial backdrop, complete with match-stick men and matchstick cats and dogs.

I continued north-westwards along the Calder Valley, following the road towards Burnley. The day was still over-cast. It was cooler than yesterday's taste of high summer; brooding grey clouds seemed to reflect the mood of the land-scape. Or was it just me? No offence meant, but this is how I always think of it 'up north'.

Riding towards Sowerby, I found myself in one of those rural stretches between the urban islands. As I cruised along, I noticed an old white milestone in the grassy verge showing the distance to Rochdale. I thought of my parents-in-law, who spent their early married life there. A photo of the milestone would be a happy reminder for them, so I turned around and motored back to take a photo. As I pulled off the main road and into someone's drive, a chap popped out from some-where and came to admire the bike. 'Yerraight, lad? Baike sounds good!' he said in fluent northern-speak and with a smile, which I took to be a good thing. I made a snap risk assessment, which included a split-second translation of his comments back into English and some first-order Doric theory analysis. I concluded that this native was friendly. I smiled back, appreciating his welcome, and rolled out my standard response of: 'Well… it's not as old as it looks. It's a Royal Enfield made in India, and it is only a year old'.

He put me right immediately: 'I know what it is, lad, I had my first Enfield Bullet in 1954'.

I'd been put in my nouveau-biker place there, but with a big friendly smile. We got chatting about motorbikes and he invited me to step inside and see his collection. These northern types are remarkably friendly towards complete strangers. I quickly re-ran the Doric theory calculations as a safety precaution – yes, I was way north of the Chester-Grimsby line, so the cordial welcome was genuine and to be expected.

This chap's immaculately clean double garage was as spotless as an NHS operating theatre. It housed a motorcycle collection as remarkable as it was immaculate. I was over-awed. I don't know my classic old bikes that well, but there was a 1961 Ariel Golden Arrow, a Suzuki 250cc, two trial bikes and a big red one – all in mint showroom condition. I tried my best to say 'wow' in all the right places as he showed me around with clear pride and I felt so fortunate that I'd turned my bike around on his drive that morning. My host, Len, must have been in his late seventies and was a Type 1 vehicle maintenance person, with slight Obsessive-Compulsive Disorder (OCD) motorcycle cleanliness tendencies. When he'd heard the throaty rumble of my bike on his drive half an hour earlier, he had been choosing which bike to take out for a spin that day. It was a privilege to meet Len; he was a proper gent and I felt humbled. But I had to be on my way, so I said my farewells. I remembered to take a photo of the mile-stone and then found my way to the A58 towards Sowerby Bridge.

A long hill leads down towards the traffic lights at Sowerby Bridge. As I headed towards the town centre, the narrow road became even more so because of parked vehi-cles. I seemed to be stuck in a queue of traffic that was hardly moving but the gap was just too narrow to risk shooting down the outside. Not that I'd do that anyway but (cough) I've seen people do it. I thought the traffic lights must be stuck on red or maybe there was a level crossing somewhere up ahead. The traffic jam freed up a bit and we rolled forwards a few more yards before stopping again. I stood tall on the bike and stretched my neck to see what was causing the hold-up.

And then I saw the problem. There was a gaggle of nine

white geese waddling down the middle of the A58. Of course there was! The traffic nudged forward again, and I rode carefully past the lazy flockers. This was absurd. Hidden under my crash helmet, I was conscious of a nervous smile. I wasn't sure if this goose sighting was normal up here or part of a sophisticated set-up. Was I the innocent party in some elaborate comedy sketch? The geese were in no particular hurry – they didn't give a hoot. They waddled along like a bunch of mates wandering down to the pub for a lunchtime pint.

A photo was a must. I had made a mistake and regretted it when I met Vincent in Lynmouth (savouring his doggy ice cream) and forgot to capture the scene. I was determined not to do the same again. No one would believe this story if I didn't get some evidence.

Pulling over to the side of the road at that point was impossible because of the traffic and parked cars, so I rode on a hundred yards until I could turn around and go back. It only took two minutes to get back, but when I returned to where I expected to find the geese, they were nowhere to be seen. I rode on further, scanning the street. Nothing. Wait a minute. Had a week on the road taken its toll? Perhaps 1,200 miles is the tipping point where the mind goes? Just then I spotted a pub called The Loose Goose – I'm not even joking. Now I was getting worried. I wondered if I was entering the twilight zone; maybe the geese hadn't been there at all. Perhaps I'd just seen the pub name and my brain had filled in the rest to make sense of the situation? Did I need to see a quack? Was it all just a wild goo— no, sorry, even I can't stoop to that one.

Turning into a small side road to gather my thoughts, I found myself parked on a bridge over the River Calder. I had a brief gander over the parapet. About thirty metres downstream, tucking into a tasty bit of riverbank weed, were nine white geese. I took a couple of photos to prove I hadn't just imagined the incident. Phew, what a relief. That side road also gave me a superb view of another of those grand old textile mills. I rode off, thankful for the diversion to see the mill, and grateful to know I wasn't going doolally, yet. Some friends and family might take issue with that.

The locals are proud of their unlikely avian residents and at the time of my writing this, the birds even have their own Facebook page with over two-and-a-half thousand followers (try searching Facebook for the Sowerby Bridge Geese).

My ride took me through a repeating pattern of small urban islands that floated in a sea of green fields and moorland. The landscape was opening up more now and I was riding through longer and longer semi-rural stretches.

Before I knew it, I was entering the old market town of Hebden Bridge. The town developed centuries ago at the point where the old Halifax to Burnley packhorse route crossed the River Hebden. I liked Hebden Bridge. On my way into the town, I scanned the buildings to find evidence of the textile industry for which it was once famous. I saw none. The trade was still going strong when John Hillaby passed through in 1966. He wrote how he heard the distinctive sound of the looms as he approached the town but wasn't able to detect the characteristic noise of woollen looms. He was soon put right by the locals who told him that in Hebden Bridge he'd only find 'cords and blewits'. That translates to corduroy and bluettes. Corduroys are ribbed cotton trousers, still quite common today, while bluette was the name given to a material once used for boiler suits and dungarees.

Back in the 19th century the soft water and fast-flowing streams of this part of Yorkshire were ideally suited to the production of a heavy cotton material called Fustian, not to be confused with the Glaswegian dialect word that means winner, first in a series, or original. The word is derived from the Latin word *fustaneum*. The trouser makers of Hebden Bridge made great strides, and the town was given the nicknames of Fustianopolis and Trouser Town. At its peak, it produced a million pairs of trousers per year. The Fustian cutter sundial statue in the town centre celebrates those glory days and, when I was there, it was doubling up as a climbing frame for the local kids. By the time John Hillaby passed through Hebden Bridge, the sun had long set on those boom days, but there were at least four weaving sheds, three dye houses and over twenty-five separate manufacturers still at work. It's hard to find them now and I didn't have the time to go looking for them. But at least two companies still produce cords and moleskin. One of those was established as recently as 2016, using a crowd-funding website. Its branding leans heavily on the northern textile tradition and it provides an impressive example of how towns can survive by using local traditions and being innovative.

Once I'd parked my bright cream Royal Enfield pack-horse, I looked around for a café for a quiet rest and somewhere to take in the Hebden Bridge vibe. For a few minutes, I became the packhorse again as I carried my panniers down the road, scanning the shops to assess how this town was coping in the 21st-century battle of the high street. People were hustling and bustling, and the place had a vibrant feel. I passed a Turkish barbers and phone unlocking shop. You'll find those on most modern high streets but there was also a higher than average percentage of prime quality, quirky and interesting individual shops. I saw upmarket places like a wine and cheesery, organic farm shops, vegetarian cafés and even a chocolate shop. There was a certain bohemian atmosphere which struck me as interesting and I quite liked it. OK, it's not quite Chagford, but there was something good going on. I found a café and a seat and stashed my panniers and helmet on the bench next to me.

A loud and extrovert waitress, who I guessed was in her late teens, bustled around between tables, broadcasting effort-less Yorkshire banter as a non-optional side dish to the snacks and drinks she was delivering. She was a gregarious young lass, all cleavage, heavy eyebrows and slashed jeans. Slightly on the ample side maybe, but on her, any excess was attrac-tively distributed. Her stand-up comedy routine with the customers was friendly enough stuff, even if a bit intimidating for one born so far south of the Doric line. Greeting me loudly, with a Yorkshire version of the nowadays ubiquitous 'Yahraihgt?' she took my order. I thought I'd got away with it – no follow-up quips about my soft southern accent or references to over-the-hill bikers. Phew, I could now have a quiet read to remind myself about what John Hillaby had found in Hebden. I wondered what the old trouser makers of Hebden would have said about the waitress's jeans. They were probably manufactured in Asia and distressed before purchase to look cool. Denim jeans seem to have superseded trouser town's high-quality moleskin kecks of yesteryear. My waitress returned after a couple of minutes with my order and I braced myself in case she'd been thinking up some killer one-liners to disseminate to the rest of the café at my expense.

Although she must have known by the obvious language barrier, she asked if I 'were local or passing through, like?'. When I told her about my ride and the tenuous reason behind it, I didn't know what I was letting myself in for. Between order taking and deliveries to other tables, she gave me the condensed history of Hebden Bridge in a rapid-fire twenty-minute local heritage primer. I wish I could have recorded it all – it was inspiring stuff. And quite an eye-opener. Before my visit, I was unaware that a few years back, the BBC had described Hebden Bridge as the lesbian capital of Britain. I lead a sheltered life. The origins go back to the hippy days, shortly after the time of John Hillaby's visit to the town. Young, free and loved-up kids squatted in the vacant housing that became available because of the industrial decline in the area. The pattern continued with the ongoing availability of cheap housing in the 1970s and 1980s. The town earned an easy-going reputation and was seen as a bohemian oasis for artists and creative people.

The relaxed social attitude was at first tolerated and then actively supported by the local council and the town attracted what we now refer to as the lesbian, gay, bisexual and transgender (LGBT) community. In between delivering the cappuccinos and flat whites to other tables, my part-time local historian told me that once the reputation had been established, it attracted more LGBT people to the town. Nowadays, Hebden Bridge is said to have a higher concentration of lesbians in the population than London or Brighton. LGBT life in Hebden Bridge is now celebrated with an annual Happy Valley Pride Festival. 'More to the point', I was told, 'it's a place where everyone feels accepted and being different isn't an issue'. If she owned a feather, she could have knocked me down with it. Not that I was shocked; it was more the fact that it was so out of the blue and not quite what I'd been expecting to hear as part of my coffee-time small talk that morning. It was a splendid story delivered by a great lass. It left me thinking what a sad indictment it was of our so-called social development over fifty years that people feel the need to seek communities where they feel accepted and safe. I'm being naïve I know, but shouldn't it be like that everywhere?

I'm not sure what John Hillaby would have made of it. At the time he walked through Hebden Bridge back in 1966, homosexuality was still a criminal act. His comments about topless swimming in Newquay and the girl in Stoke without a wedding ring hint at the social attitudes of the 1960s. As a child of the 1950s myself, I remember what those attitudes were like and it seems a world away from today's Britain. I never knew John Hillaby, but I get the impression he was a well-travelled and broad-minded person. At fifty-six years old, when he did his walk, however, he had his social and moral compass calibrated in the 1930s. Attitudes to LGBT have changed out of all recognition since 1966 and while some changes to Britain since John Hillaby's walk have been negative, this is one aspect of change we can applaud. I left the café feeling suitably uplifted and would never think of Hebden Bridge in the same way again. Attuned to the diversity of the place, I noticed a few rainbows scattered around in the form of flags and signs in shop windows as I walked back to the bike.

I motored slowly out of town, still observing the signs of change and hoping to see some evidence of trouser manufacture. Damn, it only struck me then that I should have asked my friend in the café about this. When it comes to towns adapting to change, Hebden Bridge has found its unique selling point and a focus for positive development. I passed by Crossley Mill, once one of the largest spinning and weaving mills in the Calder Valley. It's now occupied by a nice-looking children's nursery. The old Rochdale canal runs alongside and is used for pleasure cruises. Yes, I liked Hebden Bridge.

A couple of miles out of the old trouser capital and I was still taking in what I'd just heard and seen – while still maintaining 100 per cent concentration on the road, of course. The weather was now looking up. Once again, my route was transitioning from urban to rural landscape and I found myself back among open fields and lush green meadows sprinkled with bright yellow cowslips and kingcups. Going through the village of Pecket Well, the sight of yet another old mill struck me. The three-storey Grade II listed Victorian building was the classic rectangular design. It was functional, built to house textile machinery and people, so there was no intention to make it look attractive – although somehow it did look attractive. It stood there as bold as brass, complete with chimney, millpond and weavers' cottages. The pretty looking former industrial complex looked like it had been dropped into an empty field. I later discovered that this iconic looking building with its stunning location and views over rolling Yorkshire countryside was built in 1887. I've morphed into estate agent speak now, perhaps the result of also noticing that the building had been developed into a range of two, three, and four-bedroom apartments. I tried to imagine the conditions of the 19th-century mill workers and how they might react to seeing these luxury apartments today. I bet those new apartments even have indoor toilets.

A former mill, now apartments, in Pecket Well

I continued northwards and the landscape became increasingly barren. Settlements thinned out and I was soon riding through sparse upland moors. That scenery didn't last for long though and sooner than I was expecting it, I was riding into Haworth. By the time I arrived, still less than twenty miles from my starting point that morning, I had come across my third Fleece Inn of the day, a reminder of what had given the area its prosperity from the 18th to early 20th century. Wool from sheep kept on the moors and water running off the millstone grit of the Pennine Hills used for washing the wool, provided the foundation for the Yorkshire textile industry. The effect of the Industrial Revolution was to shift activities such as wool combing and spinning out of the scattered rural villages and into the growing towns of the West Riding of Yorkshire.

Haworth is famous as the home of the Brontë sisters, but lesser-known claims to fame include being the world's first-ever Fairtrade village and being twinned with Machu Picchu, in Peru. I had been keen to add Haworth to my route, having visited the town for the first time with Jan the previous year. We'd visited the Old Parsonage where the Brontës had lived but this time around I was hoping to add a visit to Top Withens, a ruined farmhouse out on the wiley windy moors and thought to be the inspiration for the house in *Wuthering Heights*. By now, my cranium jukebox was providing a constant loop, Kate Bush playlist.

Stopping off at the town car park, I had another quick look at the Old Parsonage, the church, and the picturesque main street. I didn't want to stop too long because of the familiar panniers problem. I headed out of town to search for the track up to Top Withens. I got quite a long way up a farm track on the bike, which only left me the last mile or so to walk to the house. I nervously left my panniers behind while I made the dash up to the old ruins. Another time, I'd prefer to take the proper Brontë Trail from the Old Parsonage and visit the Brontë waterfall on the way, but as usual on this trip, time was tight.

My walk up to Top Withens was far too frantic; just the opposite of my Shinrin-Yoku experience in Somerset. When I finally got there, I scanned the horizon to take in the stunning views that extended for miles around, over what is now referred to as the Brontë Moors. The jury is still out on whether the 16th-century farmhouse ruin I was looking at was the inspiration for the house in *Wuthering Heights*. The appearance of the building wasn't a brilliant match, from what I could remember, but the romantic setting was.

I was back on the Pennine Way again. Although John Hillaby doesn't mention Top Withens in his book, he makes a point of talking about Wolf Stones, a significant hill about two miles further to the north. That peak marks the geological boundary between the two main heavyweight rock types of this stretch of the Pennines; the millstone grit to the south and the Carboniferous limestone to the north. I completely get why John Hillaby highlights this point. Gritstone produces the rather bleak acid bogs that form such hard-going tracks for walkers. Limestone, on the other hand, drains well and results in springy turf, beautiful wildflowers and geomorphology to die for. Anyone familiar with the limestone scenery of Malham Cove and Gordale Scar will know what I mean. It is very appropriate that the geological boundary lies at that point, on the very edge of the Brontë Moors, where Heathcliff and Cathy came together. It forms a fitting metaphor as the hard and unforgiving gritstone gives way to the soft and vulnerable Carboniferous limestone.

Before long, I was in the Yorkshire Dales National Park. I love the Yorkshire Dales. Mainly because of that stunning limestone scenery, but also because of many happy memories from previous trips there with family and friends. I'm not the only one to feel that way, it's another magnet for walkers and increasingly in recent years, for cyclists. Horton in Ribblesdale comes in at number four in the OS's list of favourite places to start a walk (after the two Peak District winners and Pen-y-Pass in Snowdonia at number three).

I had ridden through the urban conurbations of West Yorkshire and out again the other side. As I entered the open countryside again, I could take to the smaller lanes again and follow John Hillaby's original route more closely. I noticed a repeating pattern to my itinerary – Bodmin, Dartmoor, Exmoor, the Peak District and now the Yorkshire Moors and Dales. The route chosen by John Hillaby, which I was still more or less following, picked its way through the very best of Britain's open and wild landscapes wherever possible.

The Royal Enfield growled away softly as I continued to ride into more open moorland towards Malham for my overnight stop. It was beautiful scenery and even at my old codger pace, I felt it was all passing by far too quickly. It was too much to take in. I envied the slow pace at which John Hillaby had travelled. He had so much more time to soak up and absorb the changes he was witnessing as he meandered north. I didn't envy his aching legs and blisters, though.

As if subconsciously recognising the need to slow down, I paused for a break near the tiny village of Airton. Noticing a group of lapwings swooping over the tufted grass on the moors, I parked up on the verge and sat propped up by a drystone wall for a while to admire their aerial stunts. As I settled into the moment, I noticed skylarks warbling away frantically at high altitude, but it was the lapwings that were putting on the real performance. They swooped dramatically just a few feet over the tufted grass and then flew off into the distance and back again on a low altitude circuit before temporarily touching down somewhere else. They must have been trying to create a distraction, or maybe they were just freaked out by the sight of a biker and his machine. I felt guilty firing up the noisy motorbike again. I'd got quite used to the peace myself, so I didn't know what the birds would make of it.

From the textile mills of Sowerby to the beauty of the Dales via the desolate Brontë Moors, it was turning into a day of contrasts. I was reminded again of the springtime verges of Cornwall and Devon when, just short of Malham, I rode through a tunnel of white flowers. What I took to be long stretch of hawthorn hedge had grown so high that it had arched over the road and joined up with the other side to form a tunnel. The old romantic in me saw it as the perfect passageway through which a horse-drawn bridal carriage could whisk its breathless and dizzy passenger as it transported her to her marriage ceremony – slightly late of course.

I soon arrived in Malham and the sun was out! I found the youth hostel, got my bike stowed away safely and checked into my shed for the night. My overnight accommodation was one of those basic but very cosy wooden pods. I sat outside, reliving the day's ride as I looked over the map and wrote up my diary. Happiness is a man and a shed in the late afternoon Yorkshire sunshine. Paperwork and digital record-keeping attended to, I turned my attention to that emergency pork pie.

Map

9

West Woodburn

Bellingham

Haltwhistle

Carlisle

Alston

North Pennines
AONB

Newcastle

Sunderland

Penrith

Middleton-in-Teesdale

Barnard Castle

Middlesbrough

Kirkby Stephen

Reeth

Kendal

Hawes

Yorkshire Dales
National Park

Nidderdale
AONB

Lancaster

Malham

Harrogate

Overview Map

Callander

Glasgow   Edinburgh

10

West Woodburn

Carlisle   Newcastle

9

Ripon

Lancaster   Malham

8

Elland

7

Liverpool   Wash

6

Stoke-on-Trent

MALHAM TO WEST WOODBURN

I arose early after a comfortable night in my pointy shed. I made my way to the main YHA hostel building for another excellent cooked breakfast. Malham hostel was packed, as you'd expect for that time of year and the dining room buzzed with outdoor types. North Face, Berghaus and Rab logos were everywhere. Like me, these hostellers were busy getting fuelled up for their day's activities. Compared to my first few overnight stops, there was a broader age range of guests breaking their fasts in Malham. There seemed to be a lower percentage of pensioners on display, in contrast to what I'd seen, and contributed to, in other hostels. I was pleased to see some families hostelling together; it's good to get kids into these healthy lifestyle habits early doors – or early out-of-doors.

My mileage target for the LeJog trip of around a hundred miles per day was working out well. I had deliberately built in plenty of time to stop for visits, meet the locals, and keep up an extravagant intake of representative local produce. The ability to assign sufficient resources for cream tea sampling should be in every route planner's locker.

Day nine would take me up the rest of the Pennine spine of England, ending up on the very threshold of Scotland. I'd hole up overnight just south of Kielder Forest and make a Reiver-style assault on the Borders at dawn the next day.

Reivers were families, tribes and clans that straddled both sides of the English/Scottish border during the 14th to late 17th centuries. They lived in turbulent frontier times, akin to the Wild West at its ungoverned and anarchic worst. Cattle rustling seems to have been an economic survival tactic of necessity. Reivers supplemented bovine liberation skills with constant inter-family feuding, much murder, ample arson and plenty of pillaging. Several hundred years of Scandinavian knowledge transfer probably left the locals with the right skill set to develop that way of life, encouraged by next to zero law enforcement. Before the Coronavirus pandemic, the nightclub goers of the north-east could still be seen trying to keep these historic traditions going in the streets of Newcastle city centre most weekends. Well... maybe not the cattle rustling.

After breakfast, I dragged my stuffed panniers out of the pod and loaded up the metal packhorse once again, ready to leave by 9 am. Two badass looking Land Rovers were parked in the hostel car park. One had two wheels on the grass because that's what they can do. High exhaust stacks, beefed-up suspension and gratuitous spotlight capacity left no doubt about their off-road credentials. The amount of Yorkshire mud they had splattered all over their once glossy navy-blue paint jobs was evidence that these guys didn't mess around.

As I pulled out of the car park and passed these two behemoths of the four-wheel-drive world, a sticker in a back window caught my eye... 'One life – live it'. These labels leave no doubt about the adventurous nature of the driver's lifestyle. Still, the pedant in me spent far too long contemplating the statement. How do they know there's only one life? It's statistically probable and we have no proof to the contrary, but can you claim that with 100 per cent certainty? Like it is an evidence-based fact? Followers of at least a dozen world religions would take issue with that. I wondered if there were Hindu or Buddhist owners of badass Land Rovers driving around with stickers announcing, 'Multiple recurring lives – live them'. My train of thought took me back to a shaman I'd once met in Ulaanbaatar. She would have something to chant incomprehensibly in an ancient Mongolian language on the subject – while intermittently consuming copious amounts of milk and vodka. I shouldn't dwell on these things.

I had a busy schedule planned for day nine, and I couldn't wait to get going in that glorious morning sunshine. It was another good to be alive day; the weather was perfect, the scenery stunning and my motorcycle's rear tyre remained inflated. I wasn't going to mess with that again.

First up on my route plan was the village of Horton in Ribblesdale. The very name sends a tingle of limestone topography induced excitement running down my spine. As I headed north, I was riding through the finest of Yorkshire Dales scenery with the rounded profile of Whernside as the backdrop in the far distance. It was like a scene from *Postman Pat* (technically a Lake District resident, if I was continuing to be pedantic) with verdant fields, lots of drystone walls and prancing lambs. The brand-new foliage of the hedgerows and trees had a beautiful vivid hue, almost lime green. It said spring had duly arrived, summer is around the corner, and we're in for a few months of warm weather and some long days. I recalled previous visits I'd made to the area over the years. Two geography field trips in the Dales as a teenager had confirmed my love of the subject. As I rode through the lanes, I ran through a mental glossary of karst scenery features. Limestone pavement – check; crags – check; sinkholes – check; caves complete with stalagmites and stalactites – check. I summonsed the images and named examples out of deep memory, somehow. I had mentally scanned *Principles of Physical Geography* by John Monkhouse back in the 1970s. It was securely downloaded and filed into the appropriate directory in my brain.

My departure from the Malham area was taking place too

fast; I felt I didn't have enough time to enjoy it. As I rode through Horton in Ribblesdale and northwards along the B6479, I was surrounded by the iconic outlines of Ingleborough, Whernside and Penyghent, known as the Yorkshire Three Peaks.

The Yorkshire Dales

Anyone who has been to the area and seen those delightful hills, can picture the classic Dales scenery through which I was riding. As the bike chugged on, past more textbook limestone pavement, it was all too much and the latent geography student in me had to burst out. I pulled off the road into the gated entrance to a field, threw the Royal Enfield up onto its stand and hurdled the gate to hug some physical geography features. This may be a beautiful image, but in reality, I removed my crash helmet and clambered gingerly over a rickety old gate.

I took a few photos of some classic looking limestone pavement that displayed textbook examples of clints and grykes. The clints are the sticky up bits and the grykes are the gaps... but you knew that. Undulating fields surrounded me, each with a generous quota of prancing lambs. In the distance, the colourful annual show of wildflowers was just becoming noticeable in valleys of hay meadow. I soaked up the atmosphere of the landscape and felt a bit of Shinrin-Yoku coming over me – if that's possible, and within the rules in a non-forest situation.

The early work of sculpting the underlying limestone, sandstone and millstone grits of the Dales was done by glaciation around 10,000 years ago. The appearance of the landscape has been heavily influenced over the years by a series of settlers. Angles, Saxons, Norse and Normans have all done their bit – clearing forests, cultivating the land and introducing domesticated farming stock. Modern methods have since taken over. Throw in the Common Agricultural Policy and the increasing influence of tourism and the landscape is far different from its natural state. The Dales scenery is arguably even more beautiful, I would say, because of all that human intervention.

As if this natural beauty wasn't enough, next up on my itinerary was one of the most impressive human-made features in the north of England – the Grade II listed Ribblehead Viaduct. It has to be seen to be appreciated; it's one of those rare grand-scale objects that somehow combine practical functionality with beautiful aesthetics. That this triumph of civil engineering was mainly the result of human blood, sweat and tears adds to its wonder. The Settle to Carlisle railway line was the last railway in Britain built by manual labour, with up to 2,300 workers involved. The viaduct opened for business in 1876 after nearly seven years of construction and the stats are impressive – it is 400 metres long and thirty-two metres high, with twenty-four arches of fourteen metres span. There are eight limestone foundation blocks of one ton each, supporting 1.5 million bricks. Impressive as they are, the facts are, in some ways, a distraction. The real impact is in the viaduct's majestic sweeping appearance and the setting. I was happy to take some time to just admire the flowing lines of the viaduct in an already spectacular landscape. I was there entirely on my own that morning and had that view all to myself. Like Monet's 'Water Lilies', Pink Floyd's *Dark Side of the Moon* and Matt Le Tissier's last goal at the old Dell football ground, the viaduct is a thing of rare beauty. To that list I should add my wife on our wedding day – and every other day since, just in case she ever reads this.

The Ribblehead Viaduct

The reality of the viaduct construction was grim, however. Workers lived with their families in shantytowns that sprang up near the viaduct. Fatalities mounted over the years because of the poor living conditions, frequent accidents and sickness. Anyone like me, with the nerdy impulse to check out graveyards, should visit the parish church of St Leonard's at nearby Chapel-le-Dale. A plaque in the cemetery pays tribute to over 200 victims who died during the creation of the viaduct. It was a high price to pay.

I planned my route to go via the market town of Hawes because it was on John Hillaby's path. Although I'd seen it described as 'one of the honeypot tourist attractions of the Yorkshire Dales National Park', I hadn't factored in a proper stop and was expecting to just sail through with effortless style and indifference. LeJog plans should always be flexible, though, and it's best to expect the unexpected. Once I had spotted the Wensleydale cheese factory and visitor centre in Hawes, my original plans went out of the window – how could I resist it?

I could bombard you with a few paragraphs of cheesy facts, figures and puns, but for once I'll keep it brief. Cheese produced from the milk of cows grazing the meadows of Wensleydale has been churned out since 1150. Without wishing to come across all five-star review, the set-up at the Wensleydale cheese factory was excellent. There were cheese-making demonstrations, a viewing gallery from which to watch the genuine thing being prepared, and more dairy product information than you could shake a (cheese) stick at. As I stood in the viewing gallery gaping in amazement, they sliced up a bulk batch of creamy gooey stuff before my very eyes and added salt to separate the curds and whey. I'm not sure how I had the nerve to take a selfie at the *Wallace & Gromit* crackers and cheese display after my Land's End comments, but I did. A week and a half on the road can do that to you.

I planned to pick up John Hillaby's route again a couple of miles further on, at England's highest single drop waterfall, behind the Green Dragon Inn at Hardraw. I found the pub soon enough and made my way round to the tearooms at the back, where visitors pay to visit the falls. John Hillaby recorded the cost in 1966 as threepence, which would be the equivalent of about 55p today. It was actually £2.50 but well worth it. The waterfall was ten minutes' peaceful walk from the tea rooms, where I left my panniers. I followed the path along a narrow river valley. It led to a wooded limestone gorge, where what I was expecting to be one of the most beautiful unbroken waterfalls in England dribbled down thirty-four metres, somewhat apologetically. If it was a man, I'd recommend a prostate check.

The waterfall might warrant another visit in the winter, to

do it justice, or at least when there had been more rain. I got chatting to an elderly couple of ladies walking their West Highland terrier dogs up the path towards the waterfall. At least I think we were chatting. I was mostly nodding in agreement, as if I understood what they were saying to me in their broad Yorkshire accents. I picked up the odd bit of information. The reason for the lower than usual flow was apparently because 'It's reet drahh' and it would be no good going to wherever their sister lived because 'ther's nought ther eether'. Fair enough, at least I'd got some useful intel on local meteorology and family distribution. The dogs looked even older than the two ladies and with their slow hobble (the dogs), I wondered if they'd make it back to the start of the path. When I got back to the tearoom, it seemed rude not to grab a mug of tea and a slice of cake. I made the mistake of telling the owner about John Hillaby's book and I tackled her on the correct spelling of the village name. John Hillaby had written about 'Haudraw', which confused my satnav, whereas the village signs clearly showed the spelling as 'Hardraw'. I won't go into the seemingly unending explanation I was given, but it included a third variation of 'Hardrow'… 'which is how the name should be spelt'. Mapmakers take note.

No time to dillydally, though. Or maybe there was. Long enough for an ice cream and then on my way again, to Swaledale, the most northerly of the Yorkshire Dales. I made my way towards the Tan Hill Inn, where I had planned to stop for lunch. Shortly before I got there, I came across two farmers repairing a drystone wall. That's not something you see every day and I dare say it's a dying art. So, on impulse, I found a suitable field gateway where I could park the bike and stopped for a chat.

The farmers seemed friendly enough and were probably glad of an excuse to stop lifting enormous stones for a few minutes. The wall was about 1.5 metres high, and I was told that they would finish the four-metre section they were repairing by the end of the day. It was a painstakingly slow process, even though they had all the stones. These chaps were probably in their mid-forties and seemed very content with their work. They knew their stuff and made it look easy. I could see how the broad base had been tapered upwards to the capstones on the top. The real art seemed to be in the ability to look at the pile of stones available and somehow home in instinctively on the one that would fit the gap they were trying to fill, to within a few millimetres. I bet they were good at jigsaw puzzles. It all fitted tickety-boo; there was no need for cement or mortar. Apparently, the angle of the wall as it slopes inwards to the top is known as the 'batter'. Plenty of scope for a tongue twister there, I thought, if you wanted a bit of a bet on a better batter. Or maybe not, it's hard to say.

The two farmers and I kept each other amused for a few minutes; they told me about wall building and I told them about my LeJog trip. They also educated me about something entirely new and a subject I would never have known about had I not bumped into them – field barns. Also called cow-houses, you can mainly see them in the Swaledale area. They appeared around the 17th century. They are neat and attractive looking stone buildings used to shelter cows over the winter. Back in the days when such folk existed, the field barns provided a favourite overnight refuge for tramps. Once you've seen one, you see them all over the place (the barns, not tramps). Small talk exhausted, my farmer friends confirmed the way to the Tan Hill Inn, where I dare say they had slaked many a thirst over the years after a hard day of wall building.

In between Hardraw and Tan Hill, I rode through the picture-postcard hamlet of Thwaite and found myself back on the Pennine Way again. The village lies on a crossroads of long-distance trails where the north-south Pennine Way crosses the east-west coast to coast walk. More to the point, it was near to the amusingly named village of Crackpot. The mind boggles over the story behind that name. I thought it must be something to do with the local nutter or drug dealer. Disappointingly, it's just another of those names that have been corrupted over the years, in this case from old English and Viking origins. Crackpot's principal claim to fame isn't its name; it's a limestone cavern that contains a columnar structure formed from a joined-up stalactite and stalagmite. You reach it by negotiating the infamous Knee-wrecker Passage.

The weather had deteriorated throughout the morning, much to my dismay. Maybe back in Malham it was still Mediterranean scorchio, but as I travelled north and higher into the Pennines, the clouds accumulated, and I was even in those clouds from time to time. Whenever I became surrounded by swirling mists, I could feel a significant drop in the temperature. It was such a difference from just a few hours earlier, when I'd cruised through Wensleydale in the sunshine.

Looking rather lonely on the high moors, when I eventually came across it, and drifting moodily in and out of the clouds, was the famous 17th-century Tan Hill Inn. I had picked up the Pennine Way again and John Hillaby's route. At 1,732 feet above sea level, it's the highest pub in the British Isles and I'd bagged my second 'highest' of the trip, to go with my tree from Somerset. I'm not counting the waterfall.

County boundary changes in 1974 meant that the pub changed from being in Yorkshire to being in County Durham, but further changes in 1987 put it back in Yorkshire again. I'd heard in the Malham Youth Hostel that the pub owners were keen to return to Yorkshire because the weather was better there.

I stopped for something to eat and drink and soaked up the thin atmosphere of being in the highest pub in Britain. I had expected it to be busier, but I must have caught it on a quiet day. A middle-aged mum and her daughter sat at the next table to me. Mum was intent on living the outdoor dream, but the daughter was more intent on keeping up to date with her friends on social media. A teenager frantically tapping her thumbs on a phone keyboard is not a sight that John Hillaby would ever have come across on his walk. I can remember mobile phones only becoming commonplace in the late 1980s and smartphones appearing in the 1990s. It was the same with personal computers. As a civil servant, I remember having to write out an application on an official form to my line manager to be considered for an email account to use at work. Working with digital mapping in OS's research and development branch in the 1980s, I remember being excited at seeing the first computerised maps and satellite images, which we take for granted on our phones nowadays. John Hillaby would have found planning and following his route a lot easier if he'd had digital mapping on a smartphone back in 1966, but I suspect he would have remained a purist and still taken his paper OS maps.

Anyone below thirty years of age must find it hard to imagine the pre-digital world. How on earth were people supposed to impress their friends without a constant feed of gastro-porn images and cute kitten videos?

There are hugely important aspects to the changes being brought about by the digital age, way beyond a brief and flippant mention here. Still, as I have used the excuse of comparing today's situation with that of fifty years ago to write this book, I feel it's fair enough to bring the subject up. We now have, in many parts of the world, 24/7 access to the Internet, and there is no going back. The positive economic aspects include access to just about anything we want to buy, with the option of comparing hundreds of prices. Less positive is the influence of targeted advertising, the temptation to buy things we don't need/can't afford, and the changing face of our high streets. Almost one third of our shopping is now online. At a time of frequent referendums and elections, there is also the manipulation of voters' opinions by known and unknown parties. Severe social and mental health aspects linked to our exposure to the digital world are gradually becoming more apparent. Issues such as social exclusion, self-esteem, peer comparison, online bullying, trolling and grooming are emerging, and we can only guess at the long-term effects. In just a few years, we have become addicted to our smartphones. Like an alcoholic in denial, we all say we can stop whenever we like. It's just a social (media) thing; 'One brief look at my smartphone won't do any harm'. The slow thinking part of our brains reassures us we can control our actions; 'I don't have to look at my Facebook page if I don't want to', while the emotional quick-thinking part is saying 'Go on, look – someone might be liking you'. Emotion is winning. Most of us haven't thought it through and seen what the digital giants like Google, Amazon and Facebook are doing to us and with us. Our seemingly innocent craving for armchair entertainment, next day delivery gratification and social reassurance is being translated into terabytes of data about us. That data shows, to whoever sees it, every-where we travel, where we live and work, our gender, our buying preferences, our viewing preferences and our political leanings. Imagine what they could do with that.

The thin end of the wedge is targeted advertising that provides us consumers with increased choice and assists us to buy all those things we don't need. The more sinister end of the wedge involves mass population manipulation and polit-ical change. Like it or not, our minds are being hacked. Most of us can see all this happening but we just carry on anyway. We appear to have entered a Faustian pact with the devil who runs the digital Hotel California in Silicon Valley – we are all just prisoners, on our own devices. For one more hit on the nucleus accumbens (which gives us a positive emotional hit for things like food, sex and financial gain) we seek the social recognition rewards from our friends. And the devil gets to know all about us so they can manipulate us for social, commercial and political gain. I'm just saying – you can't check out any time you like; you can never leave.

Mum and daughter were the only other customers in the Tan Hill Inn while I was there. I had high hopes of mingling with some locals and perhaps stumbling across a modern re-run of the *Monty Python* four Yorkshireman sketch, but it wasn't to be. I had to dream one up in my head for myself when I left and rode on.

1st Yorkshireman: Who'd have thought fifty years ago we'd be sittin' here watching t' Premier League on our iPhones?
2nd Yorkshireman: Aye, in those days we'd be glad to hear' t' scores at 5 o'clock on't wireless.
3rd Yorkshireman: You were bloody lucky, we 'ad no wireless in our house, we had to mek do with t' newspaper next day.
4th Yorkshireman: Newspaper! No one were rich enough to buy a newspaper in our house; in fact, our 'ouse were a newspaper, rolled up in't gutter.
1st Yorkshireman: Bloody Nora, we could never afford to live in a gutter, we had to live in a rotten sheep carcass in't corner of t' field.
2nd Yorkshireman: We used to dream of living in a sheep carcass…
1st Yorkshireman: Aye, try telling that to the bloody millennials today.

My poor attempt at a *Monty Python* re-run kept me going for a few miles after I left the pub. As I picked up the route towards Barnard Castle, some unwelcome spots of rain hit my visor and brought me back to the present day. Although it was only half-hearted drizzle, it was enough to be a nuisance. With the weather being so disappointing and the visibility poor, I was getting worried that I wouldn't have time to see Hadrian's Wall on my way through.

Barnard Castle provided an opportunity to top up with fuel and as I did so, I noticed that I'd already notched up nearly 1,000 miles since leaving Land's End. The most direct route would have got me to John o' Groats a long time ago. I was so glad that I hadn't taken it; I'd have missed so much! The bike was proving to be frugal on fuel but without a graduated fuel gauge, it was sensible to top up reasonably frequently – I never knew when the next garage would appear, especially on the minor roads that I'd chosen for my route. I liked Barnard Castle. It had a grand look about it with a big broad market street, a river, and a castle. It even had a Specsavers.

Keeping close to John Hillaby's original route, I rode through the North Pennines AONB to Alston. From there, I headed to Haltwhistle, which seemed to be quite a pleasant market town to me, although John Hillaby described it as rather run down. The town is claimed to be the centre of Britain, although there are one or two other claimants for the title. A proper investigation into the various contenders could easily occupy another chapter or two.

Whistling ticked off while I briefly halted, I continued towards Hadrian's Wall. I'd been looking forward to this part of the trip enormously. I had researched the best places to view the famous UNESCO World Heritage Site, considered by some to be the location of the original British north-south dividing line (Chapter six, theory one). I followed signs to Vindolanda, just south of the wall. It turned out to be an ex-Roman fort – not the eat-all-you-can curry house suggested by the name. It's no good heading there after a good skinful on a Friday night in Haltwhistle. I joke, but in reality, the site is one of the most significant Roman remains in Europe. Back in Hadrian's day, this was the site of a massive Roman garrison and they manned it for the best part of 300 years, until AD 370. That's a long time – if you stop and think about it in a modern-day context, it's like the Romans going home today after being in charge of Britain since the 1700s. I did a quick lap of the Vindolanda visitor centre car park and decided it wasn't the day to visit. The drizzle was persisting and the thought of spending good money to trudge around the site in the rain wasn't appealing.

Instead, I rode up to Cawfields and Housesteads – two other famous sites that are well renowned for their excellent views of the wall. I got a few photos of the wall near to Cawfields at a spot where you can see it stretching out for miles into the distance. John Hillaby thought it looked like an enormous roller-coaster.

I had professional respect for the Roman surveyors who had chosen the position and course of the wall. They had identified a suitable ridge, extending across Britain from coast to coast, and chosen it as the optimal line to follow, taking into account the natural contours and height. In Northumberland, the wall follows the Great Whin Sill, a vast slab of igneous dolerite rock. Joining up already imposing outcrops and crags with a massive wall, up to six metres high in places, was a political statement of force as much as a practical defensive line.

The day's weather wasn't helpful for photographs, so I admired the wall in real-time instead, trying to soak up the historical vibes in the moment. I was also soaking up a lot of the Northumberland drizzle in the moment, so instead, I moved on to look for the excavated Roman fort at Housesteads. I discovered a public footpath that ran next to, and bypassed, the visitor centre. It led to the remains of the old fort. I wandered along the path far enough to get a long-range view of the fort, but the weather was still being persistently northern, so I decided a proper visit deserved a better day. Next time I'd choose a fine day, take the time to get the full tour in, and include the visitor centre. I returned to the car park, saddled up and moved on, feeling a twinge of guilt at yet again indulging in some tick-box tourism. Hadrian's Wall deserved more respect.

As I rode north-eastwards along the B6318, I glimpsed the internationally famous 'Sycamore Gap', site of England's 2016 Tree of the Year, and fifth-placed 2017 European Tree of the Year. A National Trust employee allegedly coined the name, when asked about it by an OS surveyor who was updating the map of the area. Those OS surveyors have a lot to answer for.

The rest of my day nine ride was through very picturesque Northumberland countryside on my way to Bellingham (pronounced Bellinj'n) and then onto West Woodburn, which was to be my stopover for the night. The rain dried up and things were looking up again. Somewhere along the back lanes, I came across the bizarre sight of a reconstructed full-size version of Hadrian's Wall made entirely out of matchsticks. It was a good three metres high and stretched out for at least two hundred metres. I didn't know people still did that, but one has to admire the sheer perseverance and determination required to collect that many matchsticks – in some ways more impressive than what remains of the original wall today. On closer inspection (maybe I should've popped back to Barnard Castle's Specsavers), I could see it was the output from a logging company. There were thousands of neatly-stacked, uniform-sized logs. Not matchsticks, but still impressive.

I stopped in Bellingham to check out the Black Bull pub where John Hillaby rested for a night. In his book, he described the pub, and made an interesting observation. He noticed how no-one in the pub was too worried about their long-lost ancestors being slaughtered by the Scots years ago, but a few miles over the border the situation would be completely different. An imprudent mention of English names such as Neville or Clifford could soon rouse feelings and instigate an argument. I have a few good Scottish friends like that.

Bellingham was another place I liked the look of. It had large attractive houses built from the local sandstone and shops that made you feel you'd just stepped back several decades. Bellingham is somewhere where you can still buy boiled sweets, which are kept in large glass jars and weighed out into proper paper sweetie bags.

I needed some black insulation tape for the bike – that's my level of mechanical finesse. The local ironmonger's shop, which seemed to stock everything ironmonger-related, not only had black insulation tape, but had it in different lengths and widths. One for 50p was just the ticket.

My overnight stop was on a farm just outside the tiny village of West Woodburn. The main A68 that passes the village follows the line of Dere Street, the old Roman road from York to Scotland. The friendly farm owner greeted me when I arrived at my lodgings for the night. She had kindly cleared a space in her garage, so I could keep the motorbike tucked up overnight – how thoughtful. The bike had never been treated so well. My host showed me to my quarters for the night and we chatted about the farm and the area. Paintings on the walls reminded me I was in stag and fox hunting country. My host explained that this rural corner of Britain was a little isolated from the rest of the world and maybe that was why the hunting tradition had continued longer than elsewhere.

My room looked out across lush grass farmland towards the River Rede, which was lazily meandering its way past, before contributing to the North Tyne. I was in classic sheep farming country and that means sheepdog country. Now there's a thing – it was a pleasant surprise to discover that Adam Telfer was a 19th-century former resident of West Woodburn. If you don't recognise his name, you probably won't have heard of his sheepdog, Auld Hemp. Those in the right doggy circles, however, will have come by the names, because Auld Hemp is considered to be the great grand daddy of the whole border collie breed. They have erected a plaque in West Woodford to recognise both Adam, his dog, and their contribution to the sheepdog world. I played with the dog's name in my mind. I reckoned Auld Hemp would be a suitable brand name for an aftershave for the young farmer community. 'Auld Hemp – the mark of a real country man'. OK, maybe it was another sign that I'd been on the road for too long.

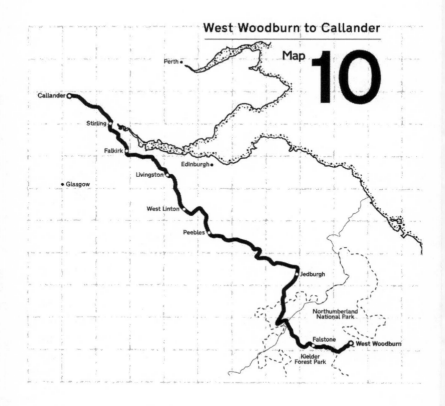

West Woodburn to Callander

Map 10

Perth

Callander

Stirling

Falkirk

Livingston

Edinburgh

Glasgow

West Linton

Peebles

Jedburgh

Northumberland
National Park

Falstone

West Woodburn

Kielder
Forest Park

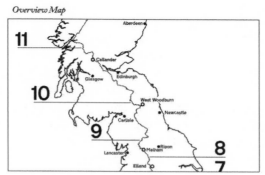

Overview Map

Aberdeen

11

Callander

Glasgow

Edinburgh

10

West Woodburn

Newcastle

9

Carlisle

Lancaster

Malham

Ripon

8

7

Elland

WEST WOODBURN TO CALLANDER

I was lying in bed in that half-awake, half-asleep state, just about aware that it was getting light outside. I guessed it was about 4.30 am and, as far as my brain was capable of decision-making, I chose to sleep on. Just then a message sound pinged out from my smartphone. I should have switched it to silent overnight or put it out of earshot. Now what? Do I ignore it or look at it? What if it was important? Perhaps Southampton FC had signed a defender at last? Damn, I had to check.

The message was from Kathrine, an American friend working in Vietnam, and she was texting to say how much she was enjoying reading the daily blog I was writing about my adventure through Britain. I mention this for two reasons: first, to make me feel good at the thought of someone out there noticing my blog (nucleus accumbens tickled) and second, for the excuse to return to discussing the point about living in a digital age and how it affected my journey. One justification for making my trip was to look at how things had changed over the years since John Hillaby walked the length of the country back in 1966. Before he set off, he did his research by poring over books and writing notes in the British Library. He had paper OS maps posted ahead in bundles for him to collect along the way, and he took two years between completing the walk and publishing the book. I guess he would have used a typewriter to write up his notes.

Things are so different in today's digital society. I had done my research at home using the Internet and I used a satnav on my motorbike to follow the route. Each night, I wrote my blog of the day's adventure and illustrated it with my pick from hundreds of images. In theory, the blog was available to thousands of viewers around the world within hours of me finishing my ride each day. In reality, I was delighted to see that over a hundred people were following my exploits… I don't know that many people. To make a book, I could cut and paste my blog content on my laptop, fill the gaps with witty banter and insightful prose and send the downloaded file off for publication and print on demand by the thousand – again, in theory. I might have been feeling good about the positive blog feedback, but I made a mental note to put my phone further out of reach when I went to bed that night.

My host at the farmhouse provided me with a splendid breakfast to set me up me for day ten – scrambled eggs with smoked salmon, toast, marmalade and tea. That would be more than sufficient to sustain a reiver for a good morning's rustling. With thoughts more on polite small talk than plundering, I enquired about the nearest big city, which turned out to be thirty miles away. It seemed weird to be told 'Newcastle… down south'. Now that just didn't sound right to me, having spent a good portion of my life thinking Geordie land was slightly further away than the northern edge of civilisation.

I got packed up and, under leaden skies, set off for the Kielder Forest with the excitement of knowing that the Scottish border was only about fifteen miles away. Kielder Forest is the most extensive man-made woodland in England – another *biggest* for my collection. The road up the side of Kielder Water was another contender for the best of the ride;

it had long sweeping bends that rocked me gently from side to side. It might have been borderline hypnotic, but the fresh early morning air had a cool edge to it and ensured I was awake and alert. I could only award 9/10 for that first section of the delightful lake-side ride because the road surface was less than perfect. Eventually, I came across a superb mile-long section that had just been resurfaced. It was as smooth as a baby's bottom and a joy to ride. If only I could take that road with me everywhere.

Kielder Water

When I stopped for a while to take a few photos of Kielder Water, the surface was like a millpond in shades of morning grey, and ghostly silent. Dropping a pin at that moment would have been deafening. As I admired the tranquil scene, half a dozen ducks disturbed the mirror-like surface of the reservoir as they glided in and silently touched down. A few ripples upset the shiny veneer, but the grey uniformity was soon restored. The new arrivals rearranged their feathers to get their landing gear back into place, had a brief confab amongst themselves, as if agreeing on an agenda for the morning, and then set off serenely on an unhurried glide around the edge of the water. An excellent example, I thought, and maybe I should take note. No more flying visits; I still needed to slow down.

I saw no one for the next few miles alongside the reservoir. Maybe I'd entered the northern Badlands or perhaps it was just still too early in the morning. It felt like I was on a proper back road and I guess it was a back road, unless you wanted to visit Kielder Water, the outdoor adventure centre or perhaps the Kielder Observatory. The latter had been on my original LeJog agenda. My initial plan for this part of the trip was to visit the observatory and camp out under what they say are some of the darkest skies in the world. The observatory is very popular, it seems, and although I tried to reserve a place well before my trip, all observatory visits were booked up for the nights when I was in the area. I know… another one to visit later.

Cruising along the next section of road, I began to feel very relaxed. The road wound northwards through the forest, with occasional views of the reservoir away to my right. I was enjoying it a lot. The jukebox in my head was serving up a steady stream of road trip backing tracks; *Easy Rider* featured heavily in the playlist, along with some Elbow and a few of the quieter Supertramp tracks. I was gliding calmly along when I came upon a section of road that was being resurfaced. That explained the pristine road covering over the previous few miles. The young lad on traffic control had one of those low-tech traffic signals – a handheld lollypop with 'Stop' on a red background on one side and 'Go' on a green background on the other side. I think he must have been bored with his one vehicle per hour pace of life that morning. The roadworks were right in the middle of a long straight section of road. With nothing in sight for at least half a mile in either direction, this mischievous highway engineer watched me approach and kept the sign on stop. He held it there, as I slowed down, until I had virtually ground to a halt, a few feet from him. Just as I was about to put my foot down, he quickly flipped the sign round to 'Go'. Ha bloody ha. We exchanged half-smile smirks in silence. His said, 'I've done you there, pal'. That's about as wild as it gets for a young reiver these days.

I noticed something interesting as I pulled away and cruised along the next section of road. Over the first few hundred miles of the ride, I was still getting used to my relatively new Royal Enfield. From time to time, I would try to estimate my speed just by the sound and feel of the bike. Nine times out of ten, I'd look at the speedometer and find I was right to within a couple of miles per hour. But heading up towards the border, I noticed a change – it seemed the forty-mph sweet spot had crept up to forty-five mph. After 3,000 miles (including the miles covered before setting off on my adventure) the engine was getting worn in and it was running smoother. Nice, I thought to myself; by the time I get home it will purr like a kitten.

An enormous road sign, plastered in stickers and travellers' graffiti, announced the fact that I'd suddenly reached the Scottish border. I somehow felt that I'd arrived before I was ready. A small but well-earned rush of excitement coursed through my veins at reaching this milestone and I had to stop and savour the moment. I set up my camera on a tripod to take a selfie, while I burst into some lively Scottish dancing next to the road sign. There was no one around that morning to witness my solo ceilidh. I think that's a good thing.

From that point on, I was into the area known as the Borders, which is characterised by drop-dead gorgeous rolling Scottish countryside. Gentle green hills and valleys of good fertile farmland, well stocked with sheep, lambs and cattle, roll on for miles around there. The Borders landscape is another one I looked back on with great affection at the end of the trip. It is some of the most beautiful countryside in

Britain. I rode on towards the towns of Hawick, Selkirk and Peebles, excited to be back in Scotland and pondering which town to stop at for a mid-morning break.

'You do not have to say anything, Mr Lamb, but anything you do say may be taken down and given in evidence'.

Of course, that's not what the local sheep farmers meant when they put out all those signs saying 'Caution Lambs'. But that's what sprang into my mind. I'm probably not the only one whose thoughts go off on tangents at the sight of signs like Mud on Road, Heavy Plant Crossing or Cat's Eyes Removed. It's funny how the brain works, or doesn't, sometimes. Maybe the twenty-five weeks on the road was playing with my mind. Next, I'd be losing track of time.

I came across a group of farmers working with a pen of lambs. I stopped a respectful distance away to watch and photograph the activities. The farmers had separated the lambs from their mums and were isolating the youngsters one by one to give them vaccinations. Once they'd been treated, the lambs were released to find their mums again. A very concerned and animated sheepdog looked on, staring intently without blinking at the lambs, knowing that he and he alone was the one who should be supervising proceedings. As they fled the pen, each lamb ran away as if supercharged, every now and again jumping high into the air – just like spring lambs.

When I arrived in Selkirk, I parked outside a building with the sign 'Grieve's Snack Attack – home of the famous Selkirk Bannock'. The shop was right next to the high street car park, at a point where the road going through the town centre widened out. It was a lucky find. At first, I'd just stopped there because it was a convenient place to park, but the sight of the Bannock shop and the seats outside turned my thoughts to sampling a coffee and cake, while I watched the world go by for half an hour. I was at last beginning to slow down to the right pace for my journey. And I was only into my third country.

The day had brightened up by now. It was warm for those latitudes and the occasional burst of sunshine was becoming more frequent. I went into the shop and was honoured to chat to the owner himself, Lindsay Grieve. He gave me the full lowdown on the history of the Bannock (a fruit loaf), the town and the local custom of beating the boundaries, known as the Annual Bussin. John Hillaby also stopped off in Selkirk to sample the local produce, which he referred to as 'the bun'. Lindsay told me that the Annual Bussin tradition goes back centuries. In brief, it seems to involve the locals riding around the town boundaries on horseback every year to check that the landowners 'haven't taken any more land, ken'. The word ken, I should perhaps explain, is Scottish for know or understand, although it seems to be thrown into the conversation liberally, especially at the end of sentences ken. I didn't ask, but Lindsay seemed to have a sixth sense that told him I needed book material and he went to impressive lengths to describe the history and social heritage of the town.

Selkirk had always been the industrial poor cousin to the more touristy Jedburgh and Melrose ''cause they've got the abbeys'. There's no textile industry to speak of now, so 'townsfolk have to go to the belt' – the urban strip of land between Glasgow and Edinburgh. Spotting my motorbike outside, he asked me about my trip and informed me that the Selkirk to Moffat road was the third best ride in the world; it was part of something known as the Borders Loop. I looked it up afterwards and found multiple references. There seemed to be a bicycle version, and I saw the motorcycle variant referred to as 'a biking nirvana which is often overlooked'. I left the delightful shop and its friendly owner to go and sample the goods. I sat outside and watched the world go by, as planned, scanning the shopfronts for any evidence of wool or textiles for which the town was once famous. Before I left, I had a quick look around the old courthouse, where the great Sir Walter Scott used to dispense justice as Sheriff of Selkirkshire in the early 19th century.

Just when I thought the weather was brightening, it changed again. The cloud cover was building up again and was becoming thicker – but I was staying dry. I decided, on a whim, to visit the village of Traquair. I thought I'd find the Cross Keys pub, where John Hillaby described an animated discussion about kilts. It wasn't there anymore, or if it was, I didn't find it, but as these things sometimes work out, I stumbled across something else – Traquair House. They say it is the oldest inhabited house in Scotland. I decide to check it out, took my time and greatly enjoyed my serendipitous find. The friendly people in the tearoom were happy to look after my panniers and crash helmet while I looked around the house. I made a mental note to reward their kindness by spending money on tea and copious amounts of local food produce when I'd finished the tour. It was only fair.

Traquair House

Said to be built on the site of a royal hunting lodge that can be traced back to the 12th century, the current Traquair House originates from the 15th century and is steeped in Scottish history. The house is a fortified mansion, but that's not far off a castle in my book and it had the grandeur and gravitas of a proper castle. Under the control of both the English and Scottish thrones over its first 200 years, the house was a key asset for the warring factions in this strategically important border area. At the time of the 1745 uprising, the Stuarts of Traquair were loyal supporters of Mary Queen of Scots and the house was the most prominent Jacobite house in southern Scotland. Bonnie Prince Charlie himself visited, as part of a meet and greet recruitment tour and as he said his farewells, the Earl of Traquair vowed never to open the main gates again until a Stuart was back on the throne. The wait continues.

No less than twenty-seven monarchs have passed through the doors of Traquair House. Mary Queen of Scots spent her last night in Scotland there before being taken south to be executed. A copy of the execution warrant hangs as a sombre reminder on a wall in the house next to a timber plaque she gave to the owner. I'm not sure that I've been anywhere else that oozed so much royal-ness.

It was time to head for the tearoom to get some perspective on things. I got chatting to a jolly Glaswegian visitor who must have been a part-time comedian... or maybe they're all like that. I wondered if he'd heard the story about the re-opening of the main gates when a Stuart was seated on the throne? He raised his eyebrows very slightly and exhaled sharply, muttering 'aye, the odds are about the same as Scotland qualifying for the World Cup again'. I'm glad *he* said that.

As I tucked into my cake, I pondered long and hard on the historical significance of Traquair House, the random privilege of class and the unfortunate consequences, throughout history, of nationalism and religion. But the cake was excellent.

As you ride along on a motorcycle, you should frequently check that everything is OK on the bike. Let's say every fifteen to twenty minutes, you should scan the instruments and routinely check temperature and fuel. On the Royal

Enfield Classic 500 there is no temperature gauge, so that's easy. And the fuel gauge is not the fancy thing you see in a car, showing fractions of the tank left holding fuel. On the Royal Enfield, the petrol gauge comprises a picture of a petrol pump that lights up when the tank is nearly empty. When the light is on all the time, there are about fifty miles of petrol left. Before you get to that point, it flashes as the fuel sloshes around the tank and covers or doesn't cover the sensor. As I made my way through 'the belt', which thankfully at that point was a fairly thin belt, the fuel light flashed. My cranium jukebox was playing a medley of Proclaimers hits at the time. I did the calculations to work out where I could refuel, based on places coming up on the route. I had enough petrol to get to Hamilton, but if there was still at least fifty miles worth of fuel, then maybe that was academical. I could get as far as Bathgate – no more.

A strange thing happened in Bathgate as I was refuelling. The sun came out and my jukebox provided the perfect Proclaimers track (if you bend the rules because it wasn't Leith). The sun showed itself for a few minutes, just teasing, then the clouds thickened again and became more menacing. A few miles out of Bathgate, the chrome protector plate on my silencer fell off, but I went back to pick it up for later repair. Protector plate – no more. My brain was still in Proclaimers mode.

Luckily, I made it to my overnight stop in Callander without getting wet or anything else falling off the bike, or me. The black insulation tape from Bellingham would sort out an emergency repair for the protector plate. I'd ridden 190 miles from West Woodford in the morning; it was to be the longest of my daily rides. And it had all been dry! Morag, who owned the cottage where I stayed that night, put the kettle on when I arrived and made a nice pot of tea, delivered with three slices of the Bannock I'd brought with me. I showered, changed and then popped back the two miles to Callander town centre for a fish supper, known down south as fish and chips. Like a delinquent biker, I sat on the kerb and scoffed the lot while the jukebox in my head played Neil Sedaka's 'Calendar Girl' on continuous loop. I reflected on the day and thought of being in the Highlands the next day and in position to begin the North Coast 500 (more often referred to as the NC500).

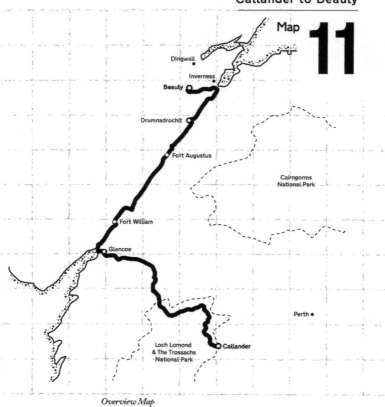

Map **11**

Dingwall

Inverness

Beauly

Drumnadrochit

Fort Augustus

Cairngorms
National Park

Fort William

Glencoe

Perth

Loch Lomond
& The Trossachs
National Park

Callander

Overview Map

13

Bettyhill
Lochinver

12

Gairloch
Beauly
Inverness

Aberdeen

11

Callander

Glasgow
Edinburgh

10

West Woodburn

Newcastle

CALLANDER TO BEAULY

'Tapps aff' is Scottish vernacular, thought to originate from Glasgow. It refers to the removal of one's shirt or other upper-body garments, usually because of hot weather, but possibly as an act of extreme emotional outpouring. For the former, this could mean, in the Highlands, blistering temperatures – maybe over eighteen degrees. An example of the latter might be fans celebrating Scottish international football success, although I'm speaking hypothetically, of course.

I mention this because when I stopped off at Fort Augustus on day eleven of *Another Journey through Britain*, it felt hotter than Death Valley. When I checked the stats in the evening, it turned out to have been a less impressive twenty-five degrees – but definitely tapps aff weather for the Highlands. The forecast for this part of the journey had improved over the last few days. Two days earlier, the outlook was dreich (gloomy, grey, wet and miserable weather... think of Wales, but with fewer sheep). Then it improved, promising just showers. By the time I got to Callander, the forecast for the next day was for lovely sunshine. You'd be forgiven for thinking I'm obsessive about such things, but it makes such a difference when you're on a motorbike. Not that I could do much to change things.

For my second Scottish breakfast of the trip, I opted for porridge and honey. My host, Morag, packed me 'ma piece' for the day, which comprised some buttered slices of the Selkirk Bannock I'd brought with me. The Proclaimers song 'I'm on my way' slipped onto the turntable in my cranium jukebox, and I *was* on my way, aha.

Callander seemed a charming wee town with a broad main street and substantial looking stone buildings, but I was through it in a flash and on my way northwards towards Glencoe. A mile or so out of the town, I rode past a gift shop and woollen mill, which appeared to be a tourist magnet. Like termites, the contents of no less than ten coaches were swarming around the shop. Passengers were re-emerging with thistle emblazoned souvenir carrier bags that I imagined to be stuffed with butter shortbread biscuits, Rob Roy tea towels and Nessie fridge magnets. I slowed down momentarily but somehow resisted the urge to stop.

I rode alongside the pretty River Fillan for a while towards Tyndrum, getting increasingly excited as I made headway into some real Highland scenery. The line demarcating the transition from Lowlands to Highlands is not so contentious as the cultural north-south line in Britain, as defined in chapter six. It is more topographically obvious, involving high ground on one side and low ground on the other. The clue is in the name. The line starts just north of Glasgow, as you approach Loch Lomond, and stretches north-eastwards up past Callander, skirting around the eastern edge of the Cairngorms and heading up to Inverness. Everything north and west of this line is the Highlands. If we want to be pedantic, and I often do, the bits around Caithness are fairly flat, but the above description is a reasonable working model to keep in mind.

Being in the Highlands again took my thoughts back thirty-five years. By 1983, I had been an OS land surveyor for nine years, but at last, I had the job that in my teenage years I thought all OS people did. I had the task of updating the

1:50,000 Landranger series, the metric equivalent to my old 1 inch to the mile favourite. That summer, I made my way up the M6 in my blue Citroen 2CV, roof down and singing a medley of Pilot and Supertramp songs out loud. I was heading for the Highlands and the beginning of a magical few years mapping Scotland. I joined a team of twelve surveyors who brought all the 1:50,000 Landranger map sheets of Scotland up to date over three and a half years. If you ever get lost using a Landranger map in Scotland... it wasn't one of mine.

There aren't many ways of getting through the Highlands by road. As you progress northwards, into ever-increasing numbers of mountains, the route options fall away rapidly. As I headed north on the A84, the options narrowed down to just two. One went north-eastwards towards Loch Tay and Perthshire, and onto the A9 superhighway. My choice took me north-west on the A82 towards Glencoe and Fort William. I followed the road to Tyndrum, where I stopped at the Green Welly café and shop, another place that was buzzing with tourists and travellers. There seemed to be hundreds of cars in the car park, a constant turnover of vehicles and plenty of touring motorcycles for me to admire. I stopped and put my Royal Enfield up on its centre stand at the end of a lengthy line of bikes so that other riders could admire it. It worked, as always. My 'old' bike always seemed to get plenty of positive comments. I went inside the café and shop to get an icy drink... oh, and another tacky sticker for the windscreen. The shop was popular; a big queue had formed at the till.

Two people stood immediately in front of me. The first was a young blonde girl, probably in her early twenties, in a primrose-coloured T-shirt and light green dungarees. It turned out she was getting away from her hometown of Swindon for two weeks' holiday. Well, you would, wouldn't you? Standing behind her was what looked like one of the tramps that John Hillaby described in his book. He was possibly in his late forties, although it was difficult to tell, and he was quite dishevelled. It would be easy to believe he'd been on the road for a few weeks, possibly months, during which time he must have been wearing the same set of clothes, which weren't optimised for the hot weather outside. His face had not seen a razor for some time. In calculating the distance he'd allowed for personal space he hadn't factored in his current hygiene circumstances and there was a less than delicate aroma of 'Eau de recycling facility' slowly wafting through the shop. He seemed a harmless guy and was keen to be friends with everyone. I wondered momentarily what set of circumstances had led the poor guy to be in his situation. Was it his choice, or had it been forced upon him? We rarely know the backstory that leads strangers to be in the positions they are, which makes it dangerous to rush to judgement, although we all do it. This modern-day tramp was trying to make small talk, in the broadest of Glaswegian accents, to the young girl in the dungarees. She was being ultra-polite and trying her best to nod in the right places. Even with my Scottish roots (by marriage), and years of living in Scotland, I had great difficulty in understanding much of his lingo. His voice was as gravelly as the path he must have travelled. The major thrust of his outpourings seemed to centre on the weather. Apparently, it wasn't right for a Scottish summer because there was 'nae wund'. He also appeared to be dispensing some health and safety advice involving midges, including a strong recommendation to purchase insect repellent, ending up with the words 'or yell ken al aboot ut'. The young girl smiled nervously and nodded, glad that it was her turn, at last, to pay at the checkout.

I took another of my minor diversions to stop off at Balquhidder church. I went to see the atmospheric 18th-century grave of Rob Roy, one-time cattle rustler, outlaw and Scottish national hero. He has been described as a Scottish Robin Hood type character. The jury's still out on that one, and again, it depends who you ask, but a 19th-century rose-tinted makeover from Sir Walter Scott seems to have transformed him from light-fingered chancer to loveable rogue, doing wonders for his reputation and his place in the romantic folk hero rankings.

Sir Walter Scott was someone, along with other Lowlander characters like Burns and Byron, who took part in a public relations overhaul of Scotland in the period between the Jacobite uprising and the end of the Victorian era. By the early 1800s, after the restoration of post rebellion order in Scotland (English view) or brutal suppression of the people (Scottish perspective), there was a political initiative to restore Scotland's place as a loyal and essential component of the United Kingdom. King George IV was the first monarch brave enough to show his face north of the border after the uprising, a mere seventy-six years after the Battle of Culloden. The king and his advisers had to choose somewhere relatively safe for the visit and thought Edinburgh would be their best bet. The Scottish capital was by then home to doctors, lawyers and academics, and to the Scottish Enlightenment: a burst of intellectual and scientific activity and achievements. Having already done an excellent job of spinning the Highland image into one of a romantic paradise in his novels, they gave Scott the responsibility of managing King George IV's visit to Edinburgh. I imagine it was like Danny Boyle getting the 2012 London Olympics gig. Scott arranged a series of spectacular events and cavalcades and people were encouraged to come along wearing tartan. Up until then, tartan was loathed by the sophisticated Lowlanders of Edinburgh. That all changed with the excitement of the visit. Everyone enjoyed the spectacle immensely and tartan was a key element in the successful branding exercise. Queen Victoria kept the ball rolling. She visited as a tourist, went on the 'sites of Scott's novels' tour and fell in love with the place. She liked it so much that she bought Balmoral. She made her staff wear Highland dress and before long the tour of Scotland was all the rage with the wealthy and influential types down south. The Highlands, with its tartan, its rugged mountains and bellowing stags, had become a brand; a shorthand representation of Scotland. What sweet irony after the banning of Highland dress in the aftermath of the 1745 uprising.

Anyway, back to Rob Roy. These days he'd be locked up or at least be subject to electronic tagging, but his life was complicated, and he seems to have had issues, especially with political loyalties. His professional robbing career took off at the time of the Jacobite uprising and he allegedly switched allegiances from time to time, happy to plunder from anyone stupid enough to offer him the opportunity. He somehow came out of it a hero – with a novel, two Hollywood films, a visitor centre and a long-distance walk all named after him.

My ride northwards towards Glencoe was just delightful and again I was left thinking how lucky I was. I had relaxed into the trip even more now. The weather was ideal, and the scenery was breath-taking. I stopped off at Loch Tulla to take in the dramatic scenery and get some pictures for my blog. As I rode on, the spectacular mountain views just kept coming. I couldn't keep stopping because I'd never get to Inverness that night… and I'd run out of film.

I use the expression jokingly, but I remember the days when you had to be very selective about getting exactly the right shot, for risk of wasting valuable film. I blast away and take hundreds of pictures nowadays because maybe 10 per cent will be good, and perhaps 1 per cent very good, if I'm lucky. Back in the 20th century, it wasn't quite the same; film had to be taken to the chemist for processing or sent away to Kodak at Hemel Hempstead, Hertfordshire. And then you had the long wait of a week or two to see what had come out – hoping that you hadn't wasted that precious film on a picture of your foot or worse still ruined everything by letting light in when you removed the film from the camera. The photographs in John Hillaby's book are grainy black and white ones and relatively poor quality by today's standards, but they remain evocative of the time.

Glencoe was everything I had remembered and more. It's such an imposing and awe-inspiring place and was at its glorious best as I cruised through in full sunshine in the middle of the day. If I had to choose anywhere on my route where I could be gifted perfect weather, it would be Glencoe. Mountains either side of the Glen towered up, getting even higher and more impressive as I entered the narrow section in the centre. I thought back to riding through Glencoe by bicycle with my sons a few years earlier and we were blessed with wonderful weather on that occasion too.

Glencoe

I was looking around for the wee whitewashed croft that features on the cover of my edition of *Journey through Britain*. There were a few candidates, but I couldn't nail one down with certainty. The sunshine was in stark contrast to the last time I'd travelled through the pass. The previous winter, I had gone through Glencoe in the snow at night with Jan, on our way home from a trip to the Highlands. We had been diverted off the A9 near Dalwhinnie as we headed south, because of a serious accident. We were told that the road would take at least five hours to clear. By the time we'd completed the diversion via Fort William and Glencoe, we realised that we would have been better off waiting the five hours.

While the scenery of Glencoe is magnificent and the climbing and walking superb, it is the massacre of members of the McDonald clan in 1692 for which the Glen is perhaps most famous. The setting enhances the drama of the historical incident and while the hard facts of the event are murky, it's clear that a wrongdoing of savage brutality took place in the Glen. The McDonald clan chief had failed to sign an act of allegiance to William III, who had replaced James II on the Scottish and English throne. The failure was possibly more one of administration than treason, according to some accounts, but in the event thirty or so of the McDonald clan were murdered. It's possible that some inter-clan score settling by the Campbells was also part of the mix. It's a sensitive topic to this day. The story is made more shocking because the soldiers sent to carry out the execution had been quartered with and shown hospitality by the McDonald clan.

The A82 continued to be a terrific road on which to ride a motorbike, and I wasn't the only one thinking so. From time to time, packs of ten or twelve bikers would come flashing past me from the opposite direction.

I was soon in Fort William and before I knew it, out the other side again and riding up the Great Glen. I decided not to stop in Fort William on this occasion, although it was another of those places that held happy memories from previous visits. I chose the quiet north side of the Great Glen as I continued my journey, rather than the faster, but much busier A82. It was the same road that I took back in 2010 with my boys when we cycled the LeJog route. It was an excellent choice; not only was it almost deserted, but it also provided the most fantastic views of Ben Nevis, which at 1,345 metres, is Britain's highest mountain. It was a real heavyweight addition to my list of extremes so far.

I had to wait awhile for boats to go through the locks at

Gairlochy, but it gave me the chance to stretch my legs, breathe in the moment, and get some more photos.

Shortly after Gairlochy, I came across the Commando Memorial at Spean Bridge. I parked up and waited patiently, sat on a grassy bank, while cars and coaches came and went. It was like my long wait by the clapper bridge on Dartmoor. I was hoping for that quiet moment when I could take a moody yet captivatingly poignant photo of the scene, unspoilt by the tourist hordes.

The Commando Memorial at Spean Bridge

As I sat waiting patiently, two fit looking lads, probably in their mid-thirties, strode up to the monument. They both wore sporty tracksuit bottoms and hoodie tops, and both carried cans of Special Brew. They had a confident swagger about them, and they conversed in heavy Glaswegian, using the foulest and crudest language you could imagine. Try to think back to the coarsest and foulest language you've ever heard. No, it was more extreme than that. What amused me was their ability to find a way of stringing extreme obscenities together with the bare minimum of non-swearing link words in a way that strangely still made conversational sense. As I listened to their banter and tales, I deduced that they were ex-marines and had seen a bit of action, mostly under the command of female genitalia with little understanding of how to command squaddies in a combat situation. As an exemplar for the use of obscene language with minimal recourse to conventional English, two well-oiled Glaswegian ex-commandos is about as good as it gets. What appeared at first sight to be two foul-mouthed yobs, however, were boys who had been sent overseas on the country's behalf to do and experience stuff none of the rest of us would ever want to see. A nasty business but thank God someone's prepared to do it. Thank you, lads.

The coaches continued to come and go, and my kilt count shot up to three, after previous sightings at Traquair and Glencoe. This latest one was rather bizarrely being worn by a German tour guide, who insisted on having his photo taken next to my Royal Enfield. It's what happens.

The riding continued to be sublime and it was quite exhilarating (in a boringly slow and safe way, Jan, not that you'll be reading this). Almost overawed by the scenery, weather and road, I had more than one hippy moment. 'Like it's all so totally freakin' beautiful, man'. Think *Easy Rider* – it's a seamless transition from Peter Fonda, Chopper Harley and a joint of marijuana to Mark Probert, Royal Enfield and a can of Irn-Bru.

The weather for the afternoon's ride was also more like the Arizona desert. OK, maybe I'm taking that already tenuous *Easy Rider* link too far now. The soaring heat forced me to pull into Fort Augustus for another leg stretch and an ice cream. I've always liked the name, Fort Augustus, by the way. I'm not sure why.

I rode on to Inverness, which seemed familiar after several trips up to the Highlands in recent years. As I approached the city, I saw a sign to Jacobite Cruises. My overactive and by now overheated imagination worked away. I envisaged a crew of blue-faced Mel Gibson lookalikes taking poor tourists out to the middle of Loch Ness, drawing their broadswords and saying, 'Now then, are we all agreed there should be a Jacobite king of Britain?'

Fortunately, by that time, I didn't have too far left to ride. It was time to get to Beauly, find my lodgings for the night, get ma tapp aff, and have a lie-down.

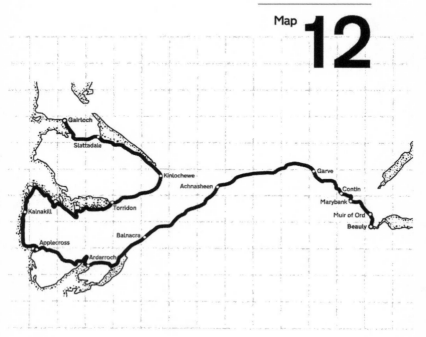

Overview Map

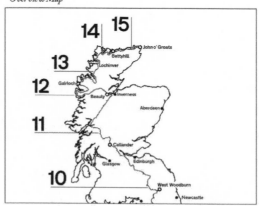

BEAULY TO GAIRLOCH

First, my feet went purple, and before I lost all feeling they turned a shade of blue and became very painful. I was at Gairloch and up to my knees in water as I headed out from the beach for a swim. When I'd arrived in Gairloch at 6 pm, it was still uncomfortably hot, especially in my B&B. The solution was to get my swimming trunks on and go for a dip. I had gingerly tiptoed barefoot across the road, over the pebbly beach and into the shallows of the North Atlantic.

When I lost all feeling in my feet, I had second thoughts about the swim and anyway, were the ladies of Gairloch ready for a James Bond moment when I later emerged, pectoral muscles rippling, out of the sea? By the time I'd fumbled my way back over a few pebbles to the shallower area, the water temperature didn't seem so Baltic after all. So, stuff it, I thought, I'm going in.

I guess my swim lasted for a maximum of two minutes (for the sake of the book this has been exaggerated by ninety seconds) before I thought about the hypothermia drill. It just wasn't worth the pain, so I called it a day and headed back to the safety and warmth of the beach. At least a dip in the North Atlantic off Scotland's north-west coast was something to tick off the to do list and an achievement I could one day tell my grandchildren about.

The thought of swimming at Gairloch seemed unlikely when I'd left Beauly that morning. It was nice and sunny back then, as I packed and saddled up, but I was expecting a deluge to arrive by midday. Departing in such benign conditions made it hard to believe the breakfast TV's weather forecast of torrential rain and thunder for later in the day – but I *was* heading to the meteorologically challenged west coast. I left early to see if I could at least get up and over the west coast's famous Bealach na Bà mountain road before the wet stuff arrived.

The day promised to be special. I was heading into what is arguably the most impressive stretch of the NC500. The roads that comprise what some people refer to as Scotland's Route 66 have been in place since 1975, when they opened the A8961 from Shieldaig to Torridon for cars. The route was labelled the NC500 in 2015. It's a spectacular circuit around the north of Scotland that has taken off in popularity in the last few years with increasing numbers of visitors each year completing the 500 miles by car, motorcycle, motorhome and bicycle. I'm sure, like LeJog, there will be visitors using all types of crazy transport to complete the route. It's only a matter of time before someone does it using a shopping trolley, hospital bed or office chair. The NC500 seems to be especially popular with groups of sports/classic car owners and I kept a tally of the makes of cars I saw as I went round. Lists – I've been told it's a man thing.

Inverness is often quoted as the starting point for the circuit, but you can begin the route at any point and tackle it in either direction. The anticlockwise option is favoured by those who say the west coast scenery is the most spectacular and so should be left until last. Who in their right mind goes around a route anticlockwise? I couldn't contemplate such an outrage to my OCD route-following proclivities and besides, I have a soft spot for Brora on the east coast, so I wanted to end up there. No, it had to be clockwise for me.

Applecross, a tiny village on the west coast, was on my agenda for day twelve and lay in wait for me about seventy miles from my starting point. That would be about the right distance and time for a leg stretch and refreshments stop. To get to Applecross, I had to go over the spectacular mountain col of Bealach na Bà, on a single-track road that is as close as we get in Britain to one of those dramatic Alpine switch-back mountain roads. With gradients of 20 per cent, the ride up to the Bealach na Bà summit at 2,054 feet, and down to sea level at Applecross is one of the steepest in Britain. It's perfect for a lung busting bicycle challenge, but not a route for the faint-hearted. I really wanted to get over the col before the rain arrived; the thought of making the traverse accompanied by thunderbolt and lightning was very, very frightening. Besides, I wanted beautiful views and photo opportunities.

As I left Beauly and headed west for a while on the main A835 Ullapool road, I passed one of those huge roadside variable message signs. This one was flashing and making sure I didn't forget about a yellow warning for heavy rain. Maybe that earlier forecast was right? My route took me through a collection of attractive settlements beginning with Muir of Ord and progressing through Garve, Balnacra and Lochcarron. I was trying my best to take my time, despite the forecast, and up to that point the weather had remained delightful. Patches of early morning mist were lifting, draped casually on the pines in places, before evaporating in the strong sunshine. It still didn't seem possible that there would be storms later.

Stopping off at Lochcarron to stretch my legs, I looked around one of the many shops selling tartan this and tartan that. A party of senior American tourists seemed to have taken it upon themselves to fund the entire Scottish national budget for 2018 by buying up every item on display. They could later remind themselves and their friends back home of their ancient Caledonian roots. I quickly checked out the kilts and other local apparel before it all disappeared. The Graham tartan is mine by marriage. My wife's great-grandfather was a travelling alcohol vendor, who in the early 1900s moved, maybe staggered, from Glasgow to Liverpool, where my mother-in-law was later born. None of this information was made available to me before I married my wife, but it may go some way to explaining our monthly expenditure on Merlot.

Somewhere along the next stretch of road heading west-ward, I saw a sign saying Slow Children Crossing. There was no one in sight, as far as I could see. I can only imagine that those kids were so indolent they hadn't even made it as far as the kerb.

A yellow Lotus 7 Caterham and a blue Mazda convertible went roaring past me in the opposite direction and my car count began. I started the official Probert NC500 sports car list, keeping a mental log of the numbers in my head and then downloading the data to my notebook whenever I stopped. Sometimes I'd have to stop anyway, just to write how many of each car type I'd seen before it became so complicated that I got the figures mixed up. You have to take these things seri-ously. I'm delighted to say that by the end of my first day on the NC500, I had seen more bicycles than flashy cars.

After Lochcarron, the road climbs and as it does, so does the wow-ometer. For the next 150 miles the rugged west coast delivers spectacular views, one after another. Rugged moun-tains spring up from nowhere, sandy beaches nestle in deserted and picturesque little coves and as I rode on, every-thing just looked picture-postcard perfect. That west coast scenery is a match for anywhere in the world – on a good day.

I got to the Bealach na Bà mountain pass by 10.30 am. Instead of thunder and lightning, it was sunny, and the views were excellent. It's a special place and once again, I took the time to park up, admire the scenery and soak up the atmosphere. I reminded myself, however, that in Scotland and especially on the west coast, the weather can be unpredictable. Ten miles up the coast it could have been different. I continued my journey down the long descent and was soon into the seaside village of Applecross. Looking across almost flat blue seas, I could see the island of Raasay and beyond that, Skye. I must have been getting the hang of things because I took my time. I found somewhere to sit and admire the view with a leisurely late breakfast/early lunch.

Approaching the Bealach na Bà mountain pass

Whoever dreamt up the NC500 gets both my hearty congratulations and my complete and utter contempt. On the one hand, it's a brilliant marketing coup and must bring so much tourism and money to places around the circuit. I saw one study that estimated that the route had resulted in an additional 29,000 visitors to the area in its first summer, generating around £9 million to the local economy. On the other hand, it brings thousands of people to an area that some of us thought was our little secret. Talking to people along the route, you hear both sides of the argument. Some complain that many tourists pass through in motorhomes, self-sufficient and not spending much money in the area. Speeding sports cars in organised convoys don't endear themselves to the locals, or anyone else. They can be a safety hazard and a disruption to all other road users when they hog all the available tarmac between passing places. Other people point to spiralling hotel and guesthouse bookings and are thankful for the boost for incomes and jobs. As with so many things, it depends on who you ask and their personal bias.

The remaining sixty miles that day were incredible; scenery as good as you could find anywhere and with perfect weather (still no sign of the rain and thunder). It was breathtaking. I just had to keep stopping to admire the views and take more photos. I wanted to slow down because it was all going too fast. I stopped from time to time for some quiet moments to soak up the scenery. Being able to experience these special times (a midge-less perfect day on the west coast of Scotland) doesn't come around often. I didn't know when I'd be back, or if the weather would ever be so favourable again. Over the day, I averaged a photo every two miles.

Beautiful little coves on the NC500

I kept thinking of my family and wishing they could have been there with me. Jan, our daughter Sarah, and her husband, James, had planned to make the trip but then, for various reasons, weren't able to. My sons, Tom and Greg, had been with me in the same area a few years earlier. I also thought about brother Bill (my big brother, not a member of the clergy) who, if he'd been with me, would have had some nostalgic flashbacks to his old motorcycling days.

The road hugs the coast and swings up to the north out of Applecross, providing plenty of opportunities to look over the sea to Skye. The pale blue water, sparkling in the sun, looked silky smooth. At one point I came across a very photogenic group of Highland cattle, all orange-brown woolly hair and horizontal horns. They were standing still, as if positioned on the verge by the NC500 marketing department. The beauties appeared to be half-asleep. A slow metronomic rotation of the lower jaw and an occasional flick of the tail were the only signs of life. They were oblivious to any passing traffic, but fortunately, when I was there at least, that was just me.

The weather was a treat, and I seemed to be in the right place. Out to sea, westwards and to the south, blue skies and sunshine persisted. To the east, however, it looked menacing; enormous cumulonimbus clouds bubbled up high into the sky. Luckily, I stayed on the right side of that dividing line all afternoon.

The views continued to astound, but despite my best efforts to take my time, it wasn't long before I was at my destination for the night – Gairloch. My pre-ride research had told me that the village goes back at least to the Iron Age when a fort was built on the headland near the golf club. I hadn't realised our ancestors had that much leisure time.

On a serious note, this strip of land bordering the northwestern coastline has been a hive of trading and raiding activity throughout history, the Vikings being especially adept at the raiding. People have lived in the area for thousands of years. The settlement pattern for most of that time, however, has been the opposite of what we see today. The fertile valleys, or straths, were used for farming oats and barley and the higher ground was used for grazing cattle. Goods were traded via the small coastal ports because it was easier to transport by sea than to go overland. Nowadays most of the inland areas are uninhabited, but the coastal villages survive, mainly through the tourist industry.

I reached Gairloch just before 2.55 pm, which I can say with some precision. When I arrived, I got chatting on the quay to someone who had just been out on a tourist boat trip. He couldn't recommend it enough. I dashed into the booking office to find out if there would be another trip that day. 'Aye, in five minutes; we go at three'. The friendly ticket seller even offered safe storage for my panniers and crash helmet. It was a deal. Luggage stowed, I climbed aboard the boat and we cast off.

A dozen other tourists made up the rest of the crew as we set out into the Atlantic in a modestly sized but reassuringly seaworthy looking boat. What had appeared to be flat calm seas when I looked over them to Skye earlier were now less flat, but nothing to worry about. It was maybe a Beaufort force four at most – small wavelets, crests glassy, occasional white horses. As our bonnie boat sped further out to sea, like a bird on the wing, the colour of the water turned to a deep cobalt blue. It provided a sharp contrast to the white of the crests as they toppled over and tumbled down in masses of foam and bubbles. We rolled around enough to let us know we were on a proper sea trip, but never alarmingly so. Looking back to the mainland, with the deep blue waves in the foreground and the mountains of Wester Ross as a back-drop, the scene was straight out of the tourist brochure.

Skipper Ian was a marine biologist, and this was no ordinary trip around the bay. We went seven miles out to sea and circumnavigated several small islands, the longest of which was the appropriately named Longa Island. As we bobbed along, Ian gave a detailed commentary on the geography, wildlife and history of the area and much more besides. For him, this was more than a means of making a living. He loved his job, and his affinity with the marine wildlife of the area was clear to see. He had put together a file containing photo identification cards for all the seabirds, so we knew what to look for and what we were looking at when we spotted something. There was a steady stream of sightings – lots of seabirds, grey and common seals and three types of jellyfish. The principal thing I took away from the trip, however, was Ian's detailed and heartfelt account of how the seabird numbers had declined so alarmingly in recent years. The amount of nesting seabirds had fallen by nearly 50 per cent since the 1980s, with food shortages, adverse weather and non-native predators being the chief reasons. Climate change is thought to be producing warmer waters, which adversely affects the marine food chain.

To avoid boring the reader with a lengthy list of seabirds and because I don't remember them all anyway, I'll just mention two of the more notable bird species we saw; Rock Doves and a Great Northern Diver. The Rock Dove is exceptional because it is the wild bird from which all the millions of pigeons worldwide are derived. It has a lot to answer for, not least of which is the distasteful job its descendants have made of our back-garden fence. You can only find the wild Rock Dove up in north-western Scotland and parts of coastal Northern Ireland. They say the Great Northern Diver is the oldest bird species on the planet. Just think about that for a moment: that's amazing. It's a winter visitor, more typically spotted in Canada or Iceland, so the single example we saw was both rare and late going home. Keeping true to its name, this one did a great dive shortly after we spotted it, to resounding applause from our boat, after which it disappeared forever.

Donna, who worked in the ticket office for Ian, had also come along for what was the last boat trip of the day. Whenever Ian stopped his commentary to tend to other things, Donna filled in the gaps with more marine-based facts and figures. The trip lasted over two hours and I enjoyed every minute. I got my luggage back from the office and Donna looked on her laptop computer to help me find my B&B for the night 'Oh aye, just doon the road'.

As I rode the short distance from the harbour up to the main village of Gairloch, the road gained some height, and I could look down to the foreshore. Taking place on the sands, I spotted what I took to be a local pastime in these parts – beach ceilidh! I couldn't divert too much of my attention to the spectacle, but on second glance I could see that it was a group of seven to eight young ladies, appropriately dressed for the hot weather, engaged in beach yoga. I rode on to my accommodation, got ma tapp aff and went for a swim to cool down.

For this leg of my journey, I've referred little to John Hillaby's route and what he found along the way. Comparisons are difficult for two reasons. First, between Fort William and Ullapool, we were on entirely different paths. He set off up the Great Glen out of Fort William, as I did, but after eight miles he struck overland to travel westwards across country. There were often no paths for him to follow. The geography dictated his route and he went for miles up this glen or down that strath, frequently diverted from his intended path because someone had inconveniently placed an enormous mountain in the way. My trip followed the roads, of course, and the indirect route around the various lochs and glens wasn't a problem on a motorbike.

Second, John Hillaby doesn't have so much to say about this part of his journey by comparison with other chapters. His book uses up almost as many pages getting from Land's End to Dartmoor as it does from Fort William to John o' Groats, although the latter distance must be about 400 miles longer. I think the principal reason for this is because the going was so severe that it was hard work just to get the trip completed, never mind writing about it. No one can fault him for that. Despite this, he battled on, describing the natural world that surrounded him. Our paths were to meet up again when I got to Ullapool.

I had travelled only 143 miles from my starting point in Beauly that morning, but somehow it seemed twice that far. For anyone thinking of riding or driving the NC500, my advice would be to allow plenty of time, take it slowly... and enjoy it.

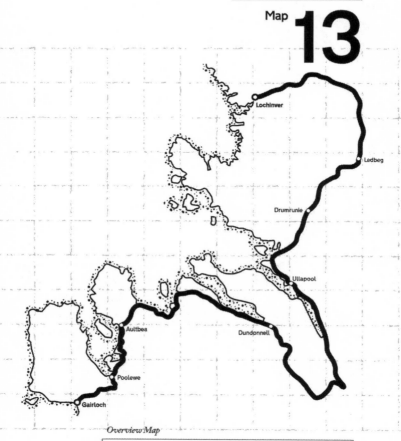

Overview Map

GAIRLOCH TO LOCHINVER

Another magnificent day's riding beckoned on day thirteen. As I went through the now-familiar routine of loading up the Royal Enfield one more time, I was briefly entertained by two local lads. I guess they must have been about five or six years old. They were riding their bikes on the gravel road in front of my B&B and out to impress anyone who was looking. They were also keeping a watchful eye on me and my motorbike. When their curiosity got the better of them, they came over to quiz me. Their opening question, with no introduction or preamble, was a textbook schoolboy one: 'How fast does that go?' Their faces visibly dropped when I told them it was 'Only about eighty to ninety mph, but no one would really go that fast because it shakes too much'.

They had been expecting much better. In hindsight, I should have nonchalantly quipped 'Oh, around 100 mph easy, but 200 mph if no one is watching'. I'd have been internally tormented by the factual incorrectness, but it's probably what they wanted to hear. Anyway, in return for letting them each sit on the saddle and twist the throttle, they rewarded me with a dazzling display of push-bike skids and tricks, some of which even involved having no feet on the pedals!

I gave them the thumbs-up and raised my eyebrows to

show how shocked I was by their audacious skills and bravery. And everyone was happy.

The previous night's Mediterranean-like weather had disappeared by daybreak, replaced by a murky and overcast, but mild day. I was expecting as much from the forecast. I was also expecting that some cloud would burn off by late morning to leave a reasonable day again. For this reason, I didn't rush to get away; it must have been nearly 10 am by the time I left Gairloch.

My route for the day hugged the west coast and promised to be exceptional. I planned to work my way up through Poolewe, Laide, Ullapool and Achiltibuie, before ending up at my stopover for the night at Lochinver. I expected the day's ride to be about 120 miles, and once again I reminded myself to slow down and enjoy it.

I considered visiting Poolewe Gardens, which I thought might be quite a sight in late May, with its rhododendrons and azaleas in full flower. The National Trust of Scotland describes the twenty hectares of gardens created by Osgood MacKenzie in 1862 as 'heritage gardens'. They lie on the same latitude as Latvia, Quebec and Alaska, but warmed by the North Atlantic Drift, the gardens contain many varieties of plants you wouldn't normally expect to see that far north. Despite the exotic stuff, it was the extensive and well-organised vegetable gardens that had impressed me most on previous visits – with multi-compartment composting facilities to decompose for. That's probably another man thing.

By the time I got to them, I decided not to stop at Poolewe Gardens. I was having a bit of a strop because the sun still hadn't appeared. Anyway, the verges and hedges along my route were already providing a spectacular floral display of their own. Rhododendrons and gorse, in particular, had painted the roadside verges in glorious purples, mauves and yellows. This was more than sufficient compensation for not visiting the Poolewe Gardens, which I'd visited several times already, and enough to give the flowery West Country lanes a run for their money.

By midday, the sun had shown itself and just as it looked like making a permanent breakthrough, it went away again. It was just teasing. Ten miles short of Ullapool it burst out as if it really meant it and then thankfully remained out for the rest of the day. It was about at this point that I came across two random road signs, about a mile apart, warning drivers to drive on the left. My immediate reaction was one of puzzlement. If our mainland European friends, who drive on the wrong side of the road, had driven to north-west Scotland, about 700 miles from Dover, surely, they'd have cracked driving properly before they got that far? In later discussions with someone who used to work for the highway authority, I was told that there are many accidents every year in the Highlands because of people driving on the wrong side of the road. The theory goes like this – elsewhere in the UK, there's plenty of traffic to remind visitors which side they should be on. Up in the Highlands, there is far less traffic. A driver can turn onto a road and see no other vehicles. Without the visual clue of traffic as a reminder, foreign drivers can unwittingly turn onto the wrong side.

As you drive up the A835 towards Ullapool, along the shores of Loch Broom, you pass through the modest settlement of Leckmelm. Maybe it would be best described as a hamlet – blink and you'd miss it. If you search on the Internet for Leckmelm, you might find references to a battle in 1586, details of the local horticultural gardens and something about holiday cottages. Leckmelm holds a special place in Scottish history, however, because it was the location of the final clearance on the Scottish mainland.

My summary of the Scottish Highlands clearances (there were also Lowland clearances) is relatively brief and given the seriousness of the events, I hope it doesn't come across as too flippant. Considerably more learned accounts of the events can be found, but the following is my concise interpretation of this sad chapter of Highland history. One thing to remember is that historically, the Highlands were far from the influences of government and the rule of law that you'd expect to find in the Lowlands. In places, they still are.

For hundreds of years, the clan system was widespread across the Highlands. The Gaelic word, clan, means family or descendants and going back to the Middle Ages, the system was mainly one in which a tribe lived in a particular area under the protection of a powerful leader – the clan chief. Clan members did not necessarily all belong to the same family, but the clans were all about relationships. Allegiance to the tribe was everything. It's like supporting Celtic or Rangers today. The chief was an all-powerful ruler over the clan territory and in exchange for providing grants of land and protection, the clan members offered labour and plenty of muscle for the endless battles with other clans. Just like the reivers down south, inter-tribal feuding was part of day-to-day clan life. In fact, the clan system is sometimes described as martial, i.e. disposed to war – which brings us back to the Celtic and Rangers fans analogy.

The reasons behind the clearances are rooted in a mixture of politics and economics, with a bit of sex and religion thrown in for good measure. Bear with me to see how that unravels. First the politics. Let's pick the story up in the mid-18th century when the Kingdom of Great Britain was united in name, but not so much in reality. By the time of the 1745 Jacobite uprising, it's fair to describe the Scots as disgruntled. They were generally getting a poor deal out of the English-dominated Westminster parliament and most Scots thought a Scottish Stuart should rule Britain anyway.

I should explain that the word Jacobite comes from Jacobus, the Latin word for James. The Jacobite uprising of 1745 was all about an attempt by Charles Edward Stuart, grandson of the exiled James II, to regain the British throne for his father, James Edward Stuart. It gets very complicated; some readers might want to fast forward a few paragraphs to the sex and religion bit.

Charles Edward Stuart, who we know more familiarly as the Italian-born Bonnie Prince Charlie, felt he had a stronger claim to the British throne (via Henry VIII's sister Margaret, Queen of Scots) than the German Hanoverians, who by then had somehow muscled in. Bonnie Prince Charlie recruited men of the Highland clans into a rebel army, gaining a battle-hardened core of warriors: quite an inspired move. Charlie's army was not all Highlanders, though. It included some Lowland forces, a regiment from Manchester and a mélange of French and Irish units. The 1745 uprising got as far south as Derby but lacking sustainable support, it ended up having to retreat and was finally defeated at Culloden, just off the A96.

This attempt had been a nasty surprise to the English ruling establishment, however, and not wanting to be caught out again, the British government upped their game north of the border. To restore order or smash the clan system and brutally suppress the Highland way of life – depending on your point of view – they built a series of forts. They constructed new roads to enable rapid troop deployment and accurately mapped the Highlands for the first time. To discourage the Scottish nationalist movement, the 1747 Act of Proscription outlawed the wearing of tartan, teaching of Gaelic and even the playing of bagpipes. The act was repealed in 1782, although personally, I think lifting the bagpipe ban was a big mistake. More seriously, in the context of the social structure of the Highlands and this rambling account of the clearances, the British government took steps to dismantle the feudal relationships and powers of the clan chiefs. The old system was changed forever. A more monetary economy developed, and the Highland ruling class gradually became more Anglicised, with a proportion of the landlords spending time down south, away from their estates.

That leads us to the economics. Highlanders were tradi-tionally mainly subsistence farmers with some limited commercial farming (and rustling) of cattle. As in England with the introduction of enclosures, the old Scottish runrig system of farming communal land gradually changed to one in which smallholders became crofters, renting farmland from a landlord. From the mid-18th century onwards, a sudden increase in the demand for wool made it profitable to put sheep on the land. Landlords had powers to evict tenants at short notice and soon vast tracts of Highland land were being 'cleared' to make way for sheep. During the sometimes brutal clearances, there was an initial migration from the Highland interior to the coasts, where some people were employed in fishing and kelp harvesting. The exact figures are disputed, but estimates suggest that at least 150,000 Highlanders were forced off their land. Many headed to cities such as Glasgow looking for work in the new factories and approximately 70,000 emigrated, mainly to North America or the Antipodes. There are stories of families being cruelly evicted without notice, occupants murdered, and farms set ablaze, but also stories of merciful landlords, who tried to help their tenants to emigrate or housed them in coastal villages.

So, where do sex and religion come into the picture? That's probably the only reason you're still reading this chapter. Well, it goes back to the 1530s and Henry VIII, in an age when, according to law, only a man could rule the kingdom. This presented a problem for the king, who despite a significant headcount of wives, couldn't find one to deliver the right result, i.e. a boy. In those days, they hadn't got their heads round DNA and the complexities of X and Y chromosomes. If a wife produced a female, it was obviously her fault, or if not, it must be God's punishment. So, although biologically Henry failed to provide that certain X factor, it was seen as the fault of his many wives. No one understood Y. When his first spouse, Katherine, couldn't produce a boy, Henry looked elsewhere. It seems he looked elsewhere quite a lot. Consumed by his stately responsibility to provide a male heir, or just incapable of keeping his trousers on – again depending on your view – Henry cut his losses with Katherine and moved on to Anne Boleyn, who was already pregnant by the king at the time of their wedding. This is where the religion bit comes into it. To enable a divorce so he could move forward with wife number two, Henry broke away from the Roman Catholic Church. Spurred on by his chief fixer and fervent protestant reformer, Thomas Cromwell, Henry declared himself the supreme head of the Church of England. A string of marriages, court conspiracies and contrived successions deprived the Stuarts of their claim to the throne of Britain – which led to Bonnie Prince Charlie's 1745 uprising. Well, that's my take on it anyway and how I managed to weave sex and religion into the clearance narrative.

To complete the clearances account and bring us back to *Another Journey through Britain* – the Leckmelm evictions, in 1880, were to be the last on the Scottish mainland. An Aberdeen industrialist bought up some land and cleared about a hundred people from their homes, but the clearance attracted a lot of bad press and criticism. The Free Church took up the cause and the case eventually led to the setting up of a Commission of Enquiry into crofting grievances. This then led to the Crofting Act of 1886, which at last provided crofters with formal rights of tenure – and that's why Leck-melm is significant.

Congratulations to any readers who read through those last few, relatively heavy paragraphs. I'll get back to a lighter tone now, but well done if you're still with me.

I rode on to Ullapool, and upon arrival I did a slow circuit of the town, looking for somewhere for a tasty, and hopefully scenic, lunch. The small but attractively formed village of Ullapool lies on the northern shores of Loch Broom, a sea loch that has for many years provided a sheltered harbour for North Atlantic fishing boats. It's close enough to the open sea to offer easy access, but far enough away to provide safe shelter. The name Loch Broom is derived from the Gaelic Loch a'Bhraoin meaning 'the lake of drizzling rain'. I imagine that's something the local tourist board doesn't talk much about.

Ullapool

I've seen Ullapool referred to as both a village and a town, and with a permanent population of only around 1,500 people, Ullapool is another place that seems to punch well above its weight. That might be because of its role as a ferry terminal for the Outer Hebrides, it's top ten ranking amongst UK fishing ports, or just the fact that there isn't much competition in that north-western corner of Scotland. Ullapool is the only sizeable settlement for miles around. When you first lay eyes on Ullapool, what strikes you is its whiteness and attractive layout. For a ferry port with a busy fishing harbour, it's easy on the eye. The British Fisheries Society built the village on a grid pattern in 1788, to a design by Thomas Telford. He got everywhere that guy; I'd bumped into his legacy of buildings, canals, bridges and roads at so many points along my route. The port initially took advantage of the herring boom of the time, but by the 1830s the boom had bust. Fishing has remained relevant over the years to varying degrees, and Ullapool remains a significant part of the UK fishing industry.

During the 1970s, the port became host to a fleet of large Klondyker factory ships, with up to seventy based in the harbour. They were mostly from the Eastern Bloc countries and took up temporary residence in Loch Broom to process herring and mackerel for onward export all around the world.

John Hillaby found Ullapool to be a pleasant little port that had changed its focus over time from fishing to tourism. And that pretty much still sums it up today, but when I visited, it was bright and bustling and I liked it.

I stopped at the Ferry Boat Inn for a late breakfast/early lunch. The establishment is a traditional looking 18th-century inn, on the busy Shore Street, overlooking Loch Broom and Ullapool harbour. I sat outside, on a bench positioned next to the wall of the inn, overlooking the sea loch. The sun was out, the prawn sarnies were tasty, and the view was fantastic – it was all delightful.

It can be amusing when you overhear little snippets of other people's conversations. It had happened to me at Glastonbury and several other places on this trip. I wasn't deliberately eavesdropping, but every now and again you hear a few sentences of someone else's chatter and you get a little window into their world. Sitting on my own outside the inn, it was difficult not to pick up some conversations of the people passing by. All right, I might have been listening. It was hard not to – and it provided added texture to the already pleasant pastime of people-watching.

A chap sat on the seawall opposite the pub was telling his partner, '...And then I just took the machine gun out of his hands, no problem'. I was desperate to hear more, but the guy must have caught sight of my jaw accidentally hitting the floor. At that moment he turned to face the sea, perhaps suddenly remembering his Official Secrets Act obligations. I missed the crucial follow-up lines. Who goes around relieving people of machine guns? Who even comes into contact with people with machine guns? Not knowing the build-up or the conclusion that book-ended the overheard snippet made it even more fascinating. Perhaps the full story would be something relatively dull – although it's hard to imagine what sort of story would make a machine gun seizure seem mundane. I could hear nothing more from the gun snatcher, so I turned my attention to a conversation between two couples who, like me, were sitting on the benches outside the inn. One couple were Scottish and from our previous chat at the bar, I'd established that the man was a North Sea rig worker, home for a bit of R&R (rest and relaxation for those of you who have never had any and may not, therefore, recognise the abbreviation). The other couple were on holiday from Canada. After the initial pleasantries concerning the weather, one of the Canadian visitors said to the local couple, 'We're not from the US, we're from Canada; have you ever been there?' I'm still not sure why no one else appeared to find it odd when the reply was, 'No, but I've got relatives in New Zealand'.

Lunch over, I had another leisurely cruise around the town on the bike and spotting a petrol station, I refuelled again just in case. Tummy and petrol tank topped up, I was on my way once more.

The next scheduled stop on my list was Knockan Crag, a name probably not familiar to many people and I must admit to my shame, I'd never heard of the place before I did my research for the journey. I took the A835 north out of Ullapool. The road followed the east shore of Loch Broom for a few miles, as far as Ardmair and then turned inland over open moorland towards Lochinver. I needed to get past Loch Broom as soon as safely possible. With its 'loch of rain showers' reputation, the sooner I was on the other side of it, the better. I didn't want to tempt fate. The traffic on this part of the route was relatively quiet. Perhaps I was just lucky. Even back in the 1960s when John Hillaby passed this way, this was already a popular destination. He describes vehicles of all types, traffic problems and road congestion. Perhaps things haven't changed so much in fifty years after all – although he made no mention of motorhomes or Ferraris.

Knockan Crag is only twelve miles from Ullapool and I was there before I knew it. When I parked the Royal Enfield in the visitor car park, two tourists came over to admire it – something I was getting used to by then. One was waxing lyrical about how the exhaust sound reminded him of his time in India, where he'd come across many similar machines. The other chap was Dutch and was highly amused by the map of Britain on my tank bag with a big arrow pointing upwards and the useful instruction 'Scotland that way'. He came over and suppressed his laughter long enough to say (sorry, this is a book, you must wait until the movie comes out to get the Dutch accent), 'You will never get lost with this navigation tool!' I told him that was all thanks to my daughter, Sarah, who was very helpful like that.

I had read that Knockan Crag was a site of discoveries as significant as Darwin's. That's quite a claim. It's all because of the unique geology of the area, which is globally famous. The rock types and structures are complex and contain some of the oldest rocks found anywhere in the world. That's gneiss. What two geologists (Ben Peach and John Horne) found in the area during their twelve-year study in the late 19th century shook the accepted understanding of the time – doing for geology what Darwin had done for evolution. The anomaly they came to study, which became the key to their revolutionary theory, was a phenomenon that defied logic. Multiple bands of rock were observed, one on top of the other. The weird thing was that the top layers were 500 million years older than the ones supposedly laid down beneath them – what was all that about? As an aside, who on earth can get their head around a time span of 500 million years?

To cut to the chase, the two geologists worked out that over millions of years, what we now know as continental drift had caused Scotland to work its way up from somewhere down near the South Pole to end up where it is today. In between, it bumped into England, separated from North America (the Appalachians and the Highlands were once joined) and was subject to constant changes because of climate and erosion. It all makes sense today, sort of, and the entire explanation is really well-presented in the visitor centre set-up at the Crag.

The highlight of a stopover has to be a walk to the Moine Thrust, where you can see the various layers exposed. The 'thrust' part of the name relates to the geological process in which the older rock layers are distorted by immense pressures into a vertical fold, like bringing your two hands together on a tablecloth, to push it up. The rocks toppled over, split and slid (thrust), so that the older layers landed on top of the younger ones. It was all a bit mind-boggling. I couldn't for the life of me work out how two chaps going around hitting bits of rock with hammers could have reached such a conclusion – and then got people to take it seriously. I decided to find out more from a renowned local geologist, Dr Nick Lindsay, who I was due to meet that evening in Lochinver. Nick and I go back over forty years, which itself feels like a geological epoch. We initially met on our first day at OS, back in June 1974, and have remained in touch ever since, despite the complex paths our lives have taken over the years.

For the next section of the ride, I went off-piste again, on a slight detour from the prescribed NC500 route. I rode out via Drumrunie to Achiltibuie, where there are glorious views out to the Summer Isles. I just wanted to see them. What a lovely, romantic name. It conjures up such a beautiful image for me – little islands floating in a turquoise sea with the sun glistening on the surface as gentle breezes caress the surface of the waves. It's probably not so appealing during a north-westerly storm in the winter. I think I like the name Summer Isles even more than I like the name Fort Augustus. I could see why the road out to Achiltibuie hadn't been included as part of the NC500 – it made some single-track sections of the official route look like the M25. The Royal Enfield chugged away as I lazily meandered through the most stunning coastal Highland scenery you could wish for, on a beautiful sunny afternoon. The thought was enough to fire up the relevant Kinks track in my cranium jukebox. That riding was surely as good as it gets.

Returning to the A835 again and heading north from Knockan Crag, back on the NC500, a magical stretch of road meanders in a wide arc through rugged scenery around Loch Assynt to Lochinver. Although that stretch of road is dual lane, a good proportion of the NC500, especially in the north-western sections, is on single-track roads... which brings me neatly to the subject of passing places.

A passing place on a single track part of the NC500

These are small lengths of lay-by that appear every few hundred yards (it's not a fixed distance) to allow a vehicle to pull over while someone passes. The theory of how this works is straightforward – you see someone coming the other way and politely pull into the next passing place to let them through, ideally with a friendly wave and cheerful smile. As I say, the theory is simple, and most people put it into practice. What's just a little annoying (see me privately for a more accurate description) is the minority of drivers who, having seen you coming, then stubbornly, or ignorantly, drive past a passing place and come right up to meet you, insisting that it's you who has to back off. It can be tourists unfamiliar with how things work, tourists who don't give a toss, or locals who resent someone else using their private road. Then there are the fleets of sports cars going around in convoy and occupying entire passing places at a time. Don't get me started on the motorhomes slightly longer than a National Express coach – bristling with satellite dishes like a mobile NASA ground station… and towing a car.

A young deer posing for tourists

I was told a story about the passing place signs by a retired Highland roads engineer. The signs are put up on metal poles, and you can see them from a distance so you can spot the next available place to pull over. Most of the signs are shaped like diamonds. They are 450mm x 450mm metal squares mounted so that the corners are at 12 o'clock and 6 o'clock, i.e. diamond shaped. They are annotated 'Passing Place', and because of their shape, they can be recognised even when they get plastered in snow, which can be a good chunk of the time between October and April. So far, so good. As from 1994, however, any new passing place sign, or replacement sign, has to be mounted to appear as a square, not as a diamond. The more astute readers will have already made the connection with the 1994 Traffic Signs Regulations and General Directions Law, which is the statutory instrument providing the legal justification for the new signs. Apparently, the change isn't as daft as it first seems. Across the whole of Europe, the diamond shape has to be reserved for providing instructions to tram drivers. New passing place signs, therefore, have to be placed in the square position to avoid any confusion with instructions to tram drivers. I'm sure the tram drivers of Sutherland and Caithness sleep more easily at night, knowing that.

By late afternoon, I'd arrived in lovely Lochinver. This coastal village is about all that's left once you get north of Ullapool – well, apart from Kinlochbervie and Durness, there's not much else on this most north-westerly stretch of Britain. It's a pleasant, borderline attractive little village. For me at least, it's just the starkness and purely functional look of the fishing harbour that stops it from tipping into the pretty category, but hey, the harbour is why the village is there. But there is a lot to be said for the place. It's well worth a visit, or even better, a stopover. Whenever I think of Lochinver, I think of the pies and the pottery. If you combine the harbour, you get a nice little descriptive ditty like Dundee's 'Jam, Jute and Journalism'. Yes, 'Pies, Port and Pottery' rolls off the tongue nicely. There you go, tourist board, you can have that one for free.

As with your house, location is everything and Lochinver wins hands down in this respect. Its nicely sheltered harbour opens out into a sea loch, unsurprisingly called Loch Inver, which itself opens out into the nearby Atlantic Ocean. A main street winds through the village down to the port and the backdrop looking inland is the magnificent Suilven, the sugarloaf shaped mountain that seems to rise vertically out of nowhere. Lochinver has a bit of a foodie reputation and the pie shop appears to be popular even on the worst of days. In fact, thinking about it, the worst of days would probably provide a wonderful excuse to head to the pie shop. I did my usual ride around the village to get the lie of the land and made my way back to the B&B that I'd recognised as I passed through on my way to inspect the harbour. This is where I'd arranged to meet up with my old mucker, Dr Nick Lindsay, that evening.

I parked up on the pavement outside the B&B and met the friendly owner, who showed me to my room for the night. I was more than a little taken aback when I saw the romantic red floral decor. I couldn't help but notice that there was just one double bed in the room. I made some polite and non-committal comment and awaited Dr Nick's arrival to find out what the hell he'd asked for when he booked the room. I know we're best friends, but this could be embarrassing. The B&B owner didn't seem at all worried. When Nick arrived, he too was shown up to the room, where I was waiting. When he entered, I saw the same perplexed and mildly shocked look on his face that I must have had when I walked in. The owner kindly left us alone to our own devices, and when Nick stopped laughing long enough, he reassured me that he'd asked for a twin-bedded room. Nick went to sort it out with the owner and soon reported back. The problem was that the owner insisted that we'd got what we asked for. Anyway, he didn't have another room available. With little other option, Nick and I had to stick with the double-bedded room. It would be just like our old camping days.

After settling in, Dr Lindsay and I set off for the local restaurant and had a splendid evening's dinner, suitably washed down with a generous quantity of the local Suilven beer. Thrusts were analysed, formations (geological and football) discussed, old times relived, and the world pretty much put to right, for one night at least.

By the time we had returned to our B&B, my thoughts

were already turning to the next day's ride. I would turn that north-west corner of Britain and head eastwards along the north coast, on the penultimate day of my journey.

We can laugh about the bedroom booking incident now and whenever we have referred to it since, we agree, 'We will always have Lochinver'.

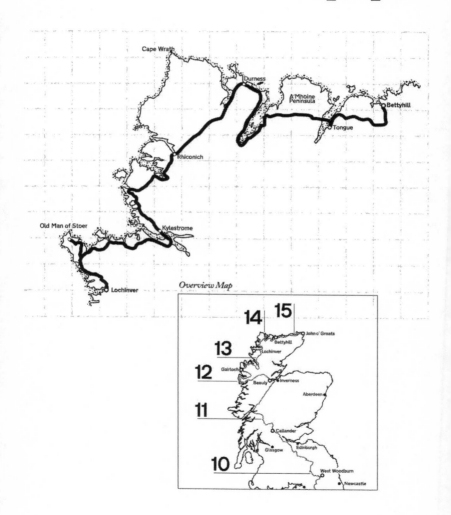

Overview Map

LOCHINVER TO BETTYHILL

Having not had a cooked breakfast for the previous couple of days, it was a treat to have one again in Lochinver. Our host pulled out all the stops with what I should describe as a full Great British, containing enough sustenance to keep us going for at least a fortnight. Dr Nick and I said our farewells to each other and vowed not to leave it so long before we met up again – so we scheduled our next reunion for the following day, at his home in Brora, after I'd completed my visit to John o' Groats.

It was the penultimate day of my end to end adventure and I was heading for the north-west corner of Britain before meandering across the northern coastline to my overnight stop at the charmingly named village of Bettyhill. I was expecting to cover around 120 miles again and the weather looked perfect.

I headed out of the village to pick up the NC500 route again, but not before I'd made my way to the pottery in Lochinver, passing a local deer on the way. In case this ever becomes an audiobook, I should point out I was referring to a red deer (Cervus elaphus), not an elderly female member of the community. Apparently, the deer are getting bold and this one seemed to have no problem with me coming up close to take a selfie. Maybe the NC500 marketing team had been out again that morning, positioning photogenic wildlife for any tourists passing through the village.

Lochinver Pottery is the home of Highland Stoneware. It's a pleasant place to drop in and have a look around. The pottery has a nice feel to it and the individually painted hand-made pieces are created by craftspeople who live in the community. You can see them working and have a wee chat with them while they go about their business.

I continued my route along the NC500 but armed with a 'sight not to miss' recommendation, I went off on yet another detour to visit the Point of Stoer. I'm so pleased that I did. It's a fantastic place to visit and I can recommend the diversion from the main NC500 route. I could have stayed there for hours. The headland was wild and rugged and provided magnificent views of the cliffs, the bird life, and the ocean, which was rumbling away about 150 feet below me.

The lighthouse at the Point of Stoer

The classic white lighthouse, another one from the prolific Stevenson brothers' production line, was completed in 1870. It marks the entrance to the Minch – the sea strait separating the north-western Scottish mainland from the Outer Hebrides. A noticeboard on the whitewashed wall surrounding the old lighthouse told me it was possible to rent a room there and I made a mental note to do more research on the subject. What an incredible place to get away from it all for a few days. It would make a fantastic writer's retreat or even a fantastic retreat for a writer. I need to work on that.

The Minch is considered to be the site of Britain's greatest meteorite strike, which took place around 1.2 billion years ago. If the 500-million-years time scale of Knockan Crag is hard to understand, anything over a billion years is almost incomprehensible to most humans. To put it into a meaningful context, it's about the same time that it takes to get through to an actual person when you phone your bank. A twenty-five-mile-wide crater is under the water somewhere, although, to date, it hasn't been discovered.

I was more intent on looking upwards. The sky was BIG on the Stoer headland that day. But it was more than that; it looked most unusual. Someone had brushed wispy white cirrus clouds over a dark blue backdrop in a beautiful high altitude watercolour painting. Being made of ice, and about four miles away, the edges of the clouds were blurring into the rest of the picture. I couldn't remember seeing such a vast expanse of cirrus before and I wondered what it might herald. I've always thought they arrived shortly before a warm frontal system so a storm might have been heading my way. My old weather paranoia was coming to the fore again but there was no other sign of any bad weather happening for a while. I marvelled at the skyscape spectacle a little longer and enjoyed the moment. With one day to go, I was maybe getting the hang of slowing down at last. Perhaps I should turn around at John o' Groats and do the entire thing again, north to south, now I was in the right mindset.

As I stood atop the cliffs and gazed down at the seascape below, my cranium jukebox song of the moment changed tracks from 'Ventura Highway' by America to the Eurhythmics' 'There must be an angel (playing with my heart)'. I considered what subliminal trigger had brought about the change. I don't think it was too difficult to work out. I was standing close to the edge of 150-foot-high cliffs, with a wimpy fear of heights. To be clear (if Jan ever gets to read this) I was nowhere near the precipice. I just included that comment in another desperate attempt to add some much-needed drama to the occasion.

As I'd seen no one all morning since I left Lochinver, I took the calculated risk of leaving my panniers on the bike and marched off on a four-mile round trip around the clifftops to meet the Old Man of Stoer. He's an impressive 200-foot-high sea stack who stands bolt upright, a stone's throw from the main cliffs, with his feet in the sea. Some nutters even climb the stack; I can't for the life of me think why. The route there and back to visit the Old Man is spectacular, especially with the far-reaching views over the Minch. The climb up to Sithean Mor (Big Fairy Hill) on either the outward or return leg of the walk is well worthwhile. Not only do you get to inspect an old OS triangulation pillar – invariably a pleasant experience – but you also see the most incredible panorama inland that includes legendary mountain names such as Quinag, Canisp, Suilven, and Stac Pollaidh. Those old OS experts knew a good place for a trig point.

After my enjoyable diversion off the standard NC500 route, I headed back to pick it up once again and continued my journey towards the north coast. As I rode back from the headland to what I suppose I should call the major road, the B869, I came across a crofter, repairing an old wall. It was too good an opportunity to miss, so I pulled up, put the bike on its centre stand so she could have a little breather, and went to chat with the crofter. His name was Hamish and straight away, he put me right on the terminology. What he was repairing was, in fact, a dyke, not a wall. It looked a lot like a wall to me, but Hamish was the genuine crofter article, so I didn't argue. Hamish gave me his full unabridged biography, covering his many years spent as a crofter. He had lived in the same place all his life, apart from a brief stint in the merchant navy. His simple croft, like thousands of others, depended utterly on subsidies. The money he got from his 150 sheep just about covered their feed. Wool was a dead loss, but he sold the rams and kept the ewes to continue the flock. I hope the relevant authorities get to read this and appreciate the need to continue funding the crofter communities.

The dyke Hamish was building was about twenty metres long and he had been working on it for three months. He reckoned it would take another two months to complete the repair. That's a top-quality dyke. What a pleasure it was to meet such a guy; his uncomplicated day-to-day life seemed a million miles from the mapping databases, positional accuracy statements, and report deadlines that were normally spinning around in my head. He got up in the morning and then, interrupted only by three meals, he spent his day building a wall, and then went to bed again. By the end of our long chat and after receiving substantial knowledge transfer, I felt competent to build my own dyke. I had taken copious notes – just in case. Combined with my experience back on the Yorkshire Moors, I must have been approaching master mason status, speciality sub-division: walls/dykes.

Armed with yet another local knowledge tip-off, I diverted off-route again to check out Kinlochbervie, and maybe also pick up a spot of lunch. The central part of the tiny village was pretty, but that's not a description anyone would use for the adjoining docks that were built in 1988. The docks were functional looking and huge. I watched a monster of a fishing boat being prepared for its next trip to sea. Its most recent catch, mostly brill, was being unloaded ready for market that evening. Typical fish landed in Kinlochbervie include haddock, monk, hake, squid and cod. The docks area looked almost deserted when I visited and had a lot of spare capacity. Back in the village, close to the harbour, I rode past the Free Presbyterian Church built in 1829 to a design by Thomas Telford. I should have kept a log of all the things I'd seen on my journey for which Thomas Telford had been responsible (yes - another list!).

The top north-west corner of Scotland is blessed with some beautiful white sandy beaches, which kept appearing as I rode onwards to my evening stop at Bettyhill. There's a danger of becoming immune to the sights as you come around a bend to yet another breath-taking beach with pristine white sand and bright blue seas. Any of these beaches would be a tourist honeypot in more accessible parts of Britain, but up in north-west Scotland, they remain quiet and often deserted. One of the most famous of these and reputedly the finest beach in Britain, although I didn't have time to confirm it, is Sandwood Bay. It may have earned its reputation and kept an air of mystery because of its relative remoteness. There's no road access to it so the usual means of reaching it is via a four-mile overland trek from the small hamlet of Blairmore, near to Kinlochbervie. I felt a twinge of guilt again at my time management but consoled myself with the thought that no matter how well you plan a trip through Britain, there is always something else to see just off the route you've chosen. It's impossible to do everything.

By the time I'd reached the village of Durness, I was on the north coast. I'd turned the corner and was heading to the finishing line along the home straight with a following wind to speed me on my way.

I didn't want it all to end just yet. There was still too much to see and enjoy. Durness is the most north-westerly village in Britain. It has a few amenities but feels 'out there' on the edge of the rest of the country. In John Hillaby's day, it would have felt even more isolated. A mile out of Durness, I rode past the impressive Smoo cave, which is a vast sea and freshwater cave system which can be explored on foot and/or boat. It was originally two caves that have joined to make one big one. The sea has eroded the limestone rock on one side, and the Allt Smoo River has attacked it from the inland side. I checked out Smoo cave on the Internet after my trip and found a website that ranked it the world's ninth most spectacular cave. The fifteen-metre-high entrance from the sea is imposing, and although ninth best in the world is quite a claim, nearly 40,000 visitors a year also think the cave system is worth a look.

My route towards John o' Groats continued eastwards, but not in the same direction for long. The A838 winds first one way then the next, seemingly in every compass direction possible. This is dictated by the topography of the area, especially the indentations made by numerous bays and sea lochs. Between the townships of Rispond and Polla, I even went south-west for over eight miles, before getting to the end of Loch Eribol and swinging north-eastwards again, back up towards the Atlantic coast.

Peat slabs drying in the sunshine

The scenery continued to be breath-taking. In expectation of more, I crossed over the River Hope and rode across the stark moorlands of the A' Mhòine peninsula. Nearly 6,000 hectares of the peninsula are part of the Caithness and Sutherland Peatlands, a conservation area scattered over 140,000 hectares of the two most northern counties in mainland Britain. This was my first sight of it. Most of the peatland is blanket bog, recognised as wetlands of international importance, and protected by various EU Conservation Directives. Most people travelling this road would notice, like me, that they were going through an extraordinary landscape. But not everyone, it seems. The peninsula has been identified as the site of the UK's first spaceport. Encouraged by a potential £3.8 billion boost to the economy, the UK government is considering spending £2.5 million on a spaceport that could be up and running in the early 2020s. Hang on a moment. Hasn't anyone stopped to think about those wetlands of international importance? Has anyone thought through how the proposed development might affect that wild and natural habitat? It's not rocket science, is it?

The thinking must be that if it's remote enough, there will be no one to complain that it's in their backyard. Maybe someone is playing the health and safety card; the result of any potential launch failure would not involve the destruction of thousands of humans – just a loud splat as the rocket dropped back into an internationally famous blanket bog protected by various EU Conservation Directives.

Pulling over onto a gritty verge, I switched off the engine and parked. I took my helmet off and looked around to take in the scene. I was determined to enjoy a landscape that, once again, I was in danger of passing through too quickly. For obvious reasons my internal playlist had already changed to David Bowie's 'Major Tom', which I sang to myself as I looked inland, over an extensive open moorland that stretched as far as the eye could see. Held about a foot off the ground by fragile spindles, bobbles of cotton grass formed a downy white sea, blown gently by the breeze... in a most peculiar way. In winter, this scene would undoubtedly be bleak... but the moors looked very different... today. I watched mesmerised for ten or fifteen minutes at the sea of cotton grass waves, happy that for once, I'd remembered my promise to myself to slow down and take in the sights before the ride was over.

I didn't have a protein pill but I put my helmet on. I continued eastwards towards Tongue, contemplating images of the moors and space rocket launches. Some people will see the imminent arrival of the UK's first spaceport as a valuable boost to the economy and a shot in the arm for the emerging UK space industry. Others will regard it as an abuse of a rare landscape that rides roughshod over the opinions of conservation experts, threatens the existence of rare biodiverse habitats, and invades the unique tranquillity of the Highland's wild areas.

Ahead of me, as I rode on in lovely sunny weather, was the village of Tongue, one of many names in the area derived from the Norse language. My mind conjured up the scene as a perplexed Viking naming committee sat up late into the night wondering what to call the place, off their faces with too many horns full of ale. Eventually, the leader of the focus group, a dishevelled looking savage, stands up and calls out (in Norse), 'I've got it, lads. Let's call this place that stands on a spit of land shaped like a tongue pointing out into the sea – "Tongue"'.

I didn't want to think too much about the reasoning that might lie behind the naming of Skullamie, the little township three miles further up the coast, but I'm guessing it involved a nuance of Nordic violence. I put those thoughts to one side and continued to meander around the coast towards my stopover for the night.

As I approached Bettyhill, I could see the twin turbines of a wind farm on the hill on the far side of the village. It was another reminder of the changing face of the landscape since John Hillaby's journey and I thought back to seeing the same thing in Cornwall on day one of the trip. That was another very windy place.

Given the exposed nature of northern Scotland, it's no

great surprise to see these giant windmills; it's perhaps a wonder there aren't even more. I was to pass many more as I progressed further east. They can be seen as a mixed blessing. They are an eyesore and a blot on the landscape for many, but to others they represent an opportunity for the future. Over 90 per cent of Scotland's electricity comes from renewable energy, most of which is from wind power, and most of that is from onshore wind farms. Part of the deal for obtaining planning permission seems to involve some kind of payback to the local community. In that respect, the wind farms have brought much-needed funding to remote Scottish communities, and all that 'free' electricity. I was told that Scottish and Southern Energy (SSE), which runs the Strathy North wind farm about ten miles from Bettyhill, makes over £200,000 per year available to local communities and charities. Bettyhill's sixty-year-old village hall is one beneficiary, for example, having been given a facelift a few years ago thanks to a grant from SSE's community benefit fund.

The Bettyhill Hotel isn't too hard to find; it's about all there is in the village (with apologies to the campsite, launderette, garage and other noteworthy establishments). I rode into the car park and hauled my luggage up to the hotel reception to check in. The reception I received was friendly and the view from the hotel was spectacular. I looked out over yet more magnificent white sands and the clear blue seas of Torrisdale Bay.

The hotel has existed since 1819, but business must have really taken off over the last few years thanks to the NC500. I found my room, showered, got changed and headed to the bar for a tasty evening meal and a couple of pints of very agreeable Orkney Gold – a local brew with a name that reminded me just how far north I'd wandered. The hotel proved to be an excellent find, in an ideal location and it was with great self-satisfaction that I congratulated myself on the brilliance of my route planning. That evening, I was joined by a party of fourteen cyclists, although I guess that would be the case on most spring and summer days. This group was having a celebratory evening meal together before the final fifty-mile push of their LeJog journey the next day. That was all old hat to me; I'd been there three years previously and done all that and got the cycling jersey. It was therefore with great smugness that I could sit back and listen to all their tales and throw my own back at them to marvel at. Tales of Devon hills, west coast rain, punctures and Scottish midges were traded back and forth, lubricated by copious amounts of Orkney Gold (other beverages, alcoholic and non-alcoholic, were available, of course). I had an enjoyable night in delightful company and that's what these trips are all about. I had to get back to the serious business the next day, when, like my cycling friends, I'd be tackling the last leg of another Land's End to John o' Groats journey.

Bettyhill to John o' Groats

Map **15**

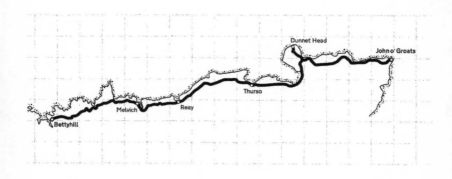

Overview Map

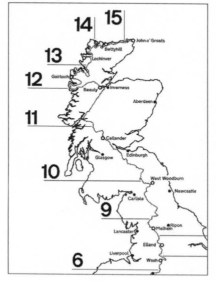

BETTYHILL TO JOHN O' GROATS

I set off from Bettyhill on yet another beautiful sunny day, at the same time as my cyclist pals. Over my final cooked breakfast of the trip, I'd also met a group of motorists, who were driving a convoy of Morgans and Porches around the NC500. We mingled in the car park once we'd checked out, taking plenty of photos and wishing each other good luck for the rest of our respective journeys. Lots of drivers wanted to get a photo sat upon a classic old motorbike – but they made do with mine. Everyone, it seemed, was doing the NC500. The cyclists were heading clockwise towards John o' Groats, on the last leg of their LeJog trip, while the motorists were heading anticlockwise to Lochinver. I should've told them to look out for the old deer.

John Hillaby described how he left Bettyhill at sunrise and scampered along the last fifty miles of his journey along the north coast. He found the scenery bleak, with scattered outcrops of worn down rock. I think by that stage of the walk, a thousand miles after setting off, he was a little worn down himself. He was probably counting off the miles with some relief. And you would by then, wouldn't you?

Just as soon as I'd got going, I diverted off the standard NC500 route again, this time to admire the stunning white sandy beach at Farr. The beautiful sheltered little cove of Farr Bay is popular with a community of people known as wild swimmers. The sun was out, and it was warm, but after my near-death experience on Gairloch beach, I was wary of those northern waters. Tiptoeing across the sand for another crotch-numbing immersion would be a step to Farr.

The beach at Farr

I took a few more photos and rode back to the A836, eastwards along the NC500. Still the beautiful beaches kept coming: Armadale, Strathy, Melvich and Sandside. I was determined not to let fantastic beach fatigue set in. They were all just so lovely; I had to enjoy every one of them.

After about twenty miles, I entered Caithness and as if following the county boundary, the landscape changed again. The bare rock of north Sutherland was replaced by more of the open moorland that I'd first seen on the A' Mhòine peninsula. The moors rolled out far into the distance, sprinkled with a dusting of bright white cotton grass.

In Caithness, they sometimes mark the field boundaries with something known as Caithness fencing – thin slabs of Devonian sandstone, standing about half a metre to a metre high. They're becoming hard to spot these days, as they fall into disrepair, crumble and don't get replaced. It's nice to come across them, though. Boundaries have been marked in the area by Caithness fencing for hundreds of years and it says a lot about the wind conditions they have to cope with. At least I assumed that's what it was – either that or the local gravedigger had an OCD-like compulsion to put everyone in straight lines around the edges of fields.

I continued riding eastward into a fresh north-easterly, along the lengthy northern coast of Caithness, through Forss, Scrabster and Thurso. The names roll off the tongue like a list of filthy Viking swearwords. Many of the place names there show their Norse origin, including Caithness itself and my mind drifted back to my mythical naming committee back in Tongue.

As I approached and went past Thurso, the landscape changed again. Rich dairy and arable farmland replaced the bleak moorlands. With the weather I enjoyed that day, I could have been back in southern England. The verges were once again full of spring flowers, every bit a match for the displays put on by Cornwall and Devon.

To the north, under clear blue skies, the Orkney Islands seemed to move ever nearer. The mainland of Orkney appeared to be almost within touching distance growing closer all the time – until I realised that I was looking at the mainland peninsula that goes out to Dunnet Head!

It was so good to visit Dunnet Head to collect a geographical extremity. The most northerly point on the British mainland was a worthy addition to the other record breakers I'd collected in the botanical, heritage and mountain categories.

As I parked up at the headland, a group of five real bikers also pulled up – all on their BMW 1200cc bikes, which seemed to be the touring bike of choice for most riders on the NC500. They all placed their crash helmets on their wing mirrors, in what appeared to be a self-assured 'nick them and your dead' gesture. So, I did the same, obviously. With silent nods, we acknowledged each other and somewhat self-consciously I tagged along behind this intimidating bunch of leather-clad road warriors as they strode purposefully towards the cliffs. I discretely checked them out as we walked along. They were all biker-talk, tattoos, swearing, bandanas and... and binoculars?

We stood silently in line at the cliff edge, staring out to sea, taking in the place's beauty, admiring the majesty of the soaring seabirds and pondering the meaning of life at this most extreme northern latitude. At least that's what I was doing. But this is when things became bizarre. One of the group, with an East Midlands accent, came out with, 'Look at that, Dave, two nice puffins on that ledge over there'. Next, I heard, 'Is that a bloody pipit on the path over there?... Yes, it chuffin' well is!'. Another lad chipped in from behind his binoculars with a slowly delivered, 'I can see plenty of cormorants out there, but what I'm really looking for is a nice shag'. The comment was met with howls of forced laughter from the rest of the group, swiftly followed by a mixture of groans, tuts and one despondent, 'Oh God, not again'. It suggested an oft-repeated in-joke – the kind that all members of the group recognised as being completely naff but accepted because of the group bonding function it provided. The penny dropped with me that these badass bikers from Burton were also keen ornithologists. They were all tooled up with state-of-the-art field glasses and bird spotting books. Sensing my incredulity, gang leader Dave lent me his 10x50s to look at the puffins. While I was observing, he gave me a David Attenborough style commentary, in hushed tones, on the puffins' seasonal migration pattern and their breeding and nesting habits. Priceless.

I kept a straight face, but inside I was bursting over this Pythonesque combination of greasy bikers and fanatical twitchers. OMG, this is comedy gold, I was thinking, and I just wanted the sketch to go on. My mind was running in overdrive as I considered how this rich entertainment could be brought to the wider audience it deserved. I dreamt up a reality TV show, to which I've given the working title, *Feathery Bikers*, and in which a disparate collection of celebrities visits some of the UK's most beautiful bird spotting locations on motorcycles. I think the idea has some mileage… and maybe plumage.

Dave and his mates were heading for Bettyhill that night, so I briefed them on what to expect at the hotel – facilities, views, food and drink, etc. I provided a full tourist guide and star rating. Some lads were only interested in what beers were available, so I told them I'd tried the Orkney Gold when I was there, and it had gone down a treat. 'Orkney Gold; that sounds like 'kin angel's piss' was the instant retort from one of the boys, without looking up from his tripod-mounted spotting scope. His snap judgement took me aback; I tried to work out whether his lightning-quick assessment reflected approval or disapproval. We moved on, conversationally and physically. We said our farewells and then all left the Dunnet Head car park on our bikes, together as one flock – me gamely hanging on at the back, at speeds sometimes approaching fifty mph, heading back the four miles to the main A836 John o' Groats road. The little single-track road was a bit of a roller-coaster and we swooped up and down gracefully like a murmuration of bikers – to keep the ornithological analogy going for maybe one sentence too many. When we reached the A836, I headed eastwards off towards John o' Groats. Dave and the boys rode west to Bettyhill for a night on the angel's piss.

Riding solo again, I soon came to the famous Castle of Mey, which was another stop-off on my list of places to visit. I was looking forward to viewing the 16th-century castle and gardens, and it gave me one last chance to spin out my adventure a while longer, before the inevitable conclusion. The staff at the castle had other ideas. They weren't keen on me leaving my crash helmet and panniers with them. As there was nowhere to leave my valuables, I had to give the most northerly castle in mainland Scotland a miss on that occasion. I bet that never happened whenever the Queen Mother used to turn up out of the blue on her motorbike.

It was a bit of a disappointment after the friendly reception I'd received everywhere else on the trip. But these things happen, and I won't hold it against them. The staff were probably only following orders. Maybe those orders were derived from centuries-old castle defence protocols warning the occupants to be wary of strangers wearing helmets – they should be treated with suspicion and repelled.

The distance to John o' Groats was dropping rapidly, and I felt myself slowing down as if I was unsure about reaching the end. I came up with one last roll of the dice, a cunning plan to spin the gig out just a little longer. I'd ride through to Duncansby Head, a few miles past John o' Groats. I'd see the impressive sea stacks and then head back to John o' Groats and the famous signpost that would signal the end of *Another Journey through Britain*.

Sea stacks from Duncansby Head

I took the A99, which runs from John o' Groats to Wick and turned onto a minor road that led me past the Bay of

Sannick and out to Duncansby Head. As the most north-easterly point in mainland Britain, the headland is the farthest point by road from Land's End and the place where John Hillaby ended his epic walk. I parked the bike in the car park, walked up to the lighthouse and then continued along a well-worn path to see the dramatic sea stacks.

I paused for a while to check out the seabirds on the hundred-and-fifty-foot sheer cliffs that form the impressively named Geo of Sclaites. Wow, that's a name, I thought; it sounded like a location in a Star Wars film. Maybe not, but the Geo of Sclaites would be an excellent place to hide a rebel X-wing Starfighter squadron.

The local fulmars were using the cliffs in the geo as their high-rise apartment block and they treated me to a spectacular aerial display. As I stood admiring them and the geological features they called home, my brain, on automatic once again, summoned up the relevant scanned files from Monkhouse's *Principles of Physical Geography*. A geo is a deep indentation in the coastline, in the form of a narrow cleft, walled on both sides by vertical cliffs. In the case of Sclaites, it's about three hundred feet long and was probably formed by a collapsed sea cave.

Standing at the inland end of the geo, at the sharp bit of the long V, I was positioned on the inbound flight path of parent fulmars as they headed home to feed their offspring. The birds' glide path brought them along the geo, below radar, on a stiff breeze from the sea. They came in fast, staying on target, to the point of the V where I was standing. As they reached me, they rose abruptly on the up-draft and made a controlled U-turn at about my head height, slowing down as they headed back into the wind to attempt their final approach to their clifftop nests. I must have been on their prescribed flight path, but they weren't going to make any unnecessary changes just because some jerk in a motorcycle jacket was standing exactly where they always perform their crucial manoeuvre. I could hear the swoosh of air as they flew within inches of my ears and they treated me to a display like watching a series of Harrier jump-jet landings. After their U-turn, the birds glided back over the geo, descending slowly towards home before pulling up sharply on the flaps to reach stalling speed right over their nests. From their full beaks, they abruptly dropped assorted fishy things into the open mouths of the hungry chicks. Well, most of the time they did. Sometimes they'd get their approach all wrong, abort and go around again, which was even more entertaining. I'm sure they blamed me for being late, when they finally returned to their nests.

I continued along the path to admire the sea stacks and then began a slow and reluctant walk back to the bike in the car park. Right, that was it; I couldn't put it off any longer. Before I knew it, I had covered the short distance to where I had to end my journey.

Fifteen days after leaving Land's End, I arrived at the village of John o' Groats. I rode out to the end of the road, to where it meets the bright blue seas of the Pentland Firth. Little white horses decorated the tops of the waves. It was a mere 1,861 miles from my starting point. That's almost a thousand miles further than necessary. You could ride both ways with that mileage, with some to spare. My meandering route was what had made it special, though. It wasn't just a quick dash to see if I could do it, or if I could complete the trip in less than two weeks. Many before me have done that. Someone will have completed it more quickly, on a motor-bike, on a Royal Enfield, and possibly blindfolded with one hand tied behind their back. I wasn't out to break any records. It was about enjoying the beautiful landscapes and fine people of Britain, and, out of interest, checking how things stacked up against the Britain of half a century ago. Taking my time, with many diversions and crazy incidents along the way, was what it was all about. Even doing it my way had seemed a bit of a rush.

I parked as close as I could to the iconic signpost, snapped the all-important photo and that was that. People weren't even on the pitch at that stage, but it *was* all over. I'd crossed the finishing line. I couldn't go any further. My Highland fling was flung. I bought the tacky sticker, had a celebratory snack and took a few more pictures to record the occasion.

John o' Groats is an unassuming place and nothing like its over-exploited counterpart at Land's End. There was a pleasant café, a handful of souvenir shops, and a car park – which was full of vehicles and free to use! I witnessed a constant stream of arrivals, including the cyclists I'd left behind at Bettyhill. Before long, a lengthy line of more cyclists, motorcyclists and people in flashy sports cars were all queuing up for their photo, standing next to the famous signpost (Land's End 874 miles), to mark the end of their own unique journeys. There were lots of smiles, handshakes, hugs, back-slapping, and lingering emotional kisses – and I hardly knew any of them.

I sat for a while in the café opposite the signpost, sipping coffee and watching people deal with the curtain falling on their own personal dramas. There was a range of reactions: some ecstatic, some triumphant and some quiet and reflective. Those people had experienced their own unique journeys, and the end meant different things to each of them. I thought back to John Hillaby and how he must have felt when he got to John o' Groats back in 1966. Tired... elated... satisfied. Who knows? In his book, he was delighted with his achievement but reflected on parts of the journey that he wouldn't want to do again. He hadn't enjoyed the rain, mist and bogs of Dartmoor, for example, and the Highlands had been a challenge. He also speculated on how good it would have been to have access to a car from time to time. But he acknowledged that it would have resulted in a completely different journey. In the closing paragraphs, he highlights how he found parts of Britain inexpressibly beautiful. Yes, I'll drink to that. They still are.

Everyone arriving at the finishing line of their end to end

journey will have that sweet moment of satisfaction, but for most people it's a bitter-sweet conclusion. There's the emotion of completing something special, by whatever means, but also the sadness of realising the adventure is over. That's how it felt for me as I sat watching the procession of finishers at the signpost opposite me. It had gone too quickly, but then I remembered thinking the same thing after taking three weeks to cycle LeJog in 2010. John Hillaby even thought the same after taking three months to walk it.

At the time you cross the finishing line there's still a lot to think about: the logistics of getting home, the tiredness, and the uneasy thought of going back to normal life with all the baggage of responsibility that involves. It's only weeks or even months later that anyone can look back and see things in perspective and draw conclusions. Luckily, although some might argue with that, I had 734 photos, a diary and thirty-two pages of handwritten notes to remind me of what I'd experienced since setting off from Land's End in the fourth week of May 2018.

REFLECTIONS

I will not attempt any profound insights. *Another Journey through Britain* was a light-hearted reflection on a kingdom's beauty and weirdness, and some of the changes from fifty years ago. A sudden outpouring of weighty philosophical conclusions, apart from being beyond me, would be neither appropriate nor amusing. I can't wrap my adventure up, however, and stick it on the bookshelf of travel memories, without some brief reflections.

I'd set out on my trip to compare today's Britain with the one that John Hillaby experienced on his walk fifty years earlier. I'm conscious that some of my conclusions are influenced by my general life experiences, not just those from my bike ride.

In some ways, Britain seems small. It doesn't take long to travel from end to end, even along the convoluted route that I took. In terms of the changes over fifty years since John Hillaby's walk, *A Journey through Britain* can still be, I'm pleased to say, a very rural experience. In following the original route as much as I could, I avoided the main urban conurbations. Britain still has vast areas of beautiful unspoilt countryside and wild expanses of moorland and mountains. The development of our National Parks and AONB has been a very positive factor in preserving these precious places. I'm sure John Hillaby would have approved of how our long-distance footpaths and trails have developed over the last fifty years. Some have full-time staff to maintain them and the trails are well publicised, via many forms of media, including the Internet. The Land Reform (Scotland) Act 2003, colloquially referred to as the 'right to roam' is another positive development, for users of the countryside north of the border. On the downside, about a tenth of the 140,000-mile network of rights of way that crisscrossed the country for decades is now difficult to access. Many paths have been ploughed up or fenced off. Others have just grown over through lack of use.

Those localised regional accents that John Hillaby described so well are still very much in evidence despite how much more everyone moves around the country and around the rest of the world. Language changes all the time. While the number of people using the Queen's English has declined over the years, those distinct regional accents have survived and thrived, and been supplemented with increased use of estuary English and social media shorthand. Good God, you can even hear regional accents on the BBC news nowadays.

Britain's traditional industries have largely disappeared and many more besides. I'm thinking of mining, steel, textiles and shipbuilding, for example. And we all miss the cellophane factory and bras of Bridgwater. But new enterprises are taking the place of the old ones. Much is happening now with new technologies and the creative/media industries. Financial and digital enterprises are at the forefront of a thriving services sector in 21st-century Britain. Britain's energy sector has been almost totally renewed.

There is a much denser network of road transport, but we've lost much of our rail system. The government has passed responsibility for parts of the national infrastructure to the private sector and foreign ownership. Numbers attending church have declined over the years, and pubs continue to lose customers. Churches and pubs are no longer the community focal points they once were. Town centres are feeling the economic squeeze as more people do their shopping online and out of town. Some towns are coping better than others, but overall, many town centres are looking tired and sad. Farming, so much the focus of post-war government policy, has gradually changed – we have gone from subsidies to produce food to payments to conserve the environment. At least those changes have enabled the countryside to survive. The danger signs are flashing, however, with the overuse of fertilisers and pesticides, the miles of hedgerows destroyed, and loss of wildlife.

We are a digital society and there's no going back. Many people are totally Wi-Fi dependent; in touch, yet so out of touch with the rest of the world. The people of Britain do not seem so united as they once were and it feels a more polarised and divided country than fifty years ago, although taking my journey in the aftermath of the Brexit vote might have influenced that view. Despite the overall rise in living standards, it seems some have gained more than others. Regional differences appear to have been accentuated and joking aside, the north-south divide is still there – somewhere.

I was so lucky with the weather. Blessed with those sunny days and blue skies, it's hard to match the north-west coast of Scotland, the seascapes of Cornwall and Devon, the wooded Wye Valley, the gritty moorland of the Peak District and the limestone scenery of the Yorkshire Dales. To pick these examples out is maybe unfair to so many other gems. The indecent haste of my trip has left me with plenty more to see.

My recollections of the journey are a series of isolated cameo images – a montage of brief memories re-enforced by the photos from each day and supplemented by snippets of remembered conversations and other things picked up along the way. So many places, landscapes and people to remember; the YHA wardens and guests, the B&B hosts and guests and all the other random meetings that you could never predict. Whenever I set out on an adventure, I'm always worried whether 'stuff' will happen. You can see throughout the book that hardly a day passed without something amusing or downright weird happening. How does that happen? I'm not sure, but somehow it always seems to.

I think I should end with the stat attack; my last chance to make a list:

- Duration of journey: 15 days
- Average day's distance: 124 miles
- Maximum day's distance: 191 miles
- Minimum day's distance: 71 miles
- Total distance: 1,861 miles
- Fuel consumption: 92.2 miles per gallon
- Days with rain: 1 day

Thank you for reading *Another Journey through Britain*. If you have enjoyed it, I would be very grateful if you could give the book a review. If you didn't like it – don't worry, the next one will be much better. You can find out more, and register for updates on: https://mgprobert.com

ACKNOWLEDGMENTS

I'm indebted to so many people for enabling me to complete my journey and for helping me to bring my account of the adventure through to a published book. The first person to thank, of course, is John Hillaby, the author of *Journey through Britain,* both for the gift of his writing and also for giving me the inspiration to write this book. Having followed his footsteps for *Another Journey through Britain,* I now owe a huge thanks to all the owners and managers of the hostels, hotels, B&Bs (and the yurt) in which I stayed overnight, and to many others who helped along the way to make my journey so memorable. The gents of GV Bikes in Taunton, for example, kept my show on the road after a puncture in Cheddar. At the risk of only naming a few people and missing out many more who I should also mention, a special thanks to Bill for the bespoke rear luggage rack, and to Les and Arthur for their hospitality in Huddersfield. Nephew, and fellow biker, Mark was great company in Derbyshire and escorted me safely into deepest, darkest Yorkshire. The Lindsays of Brora enriched my journey enormously as I came back down the east coast of Sutherland. We'll skip over the Lochinver incident, Nick, and hope that the news never breaks out (I'll let you know if anyone ever tries to order the book).

Turning my daily blog of the ride (which, sadly, no longer exists) into a book seemed a good idea at the time. I was spurred on by a few well-meaning family members who, in their defence, probably didn't expect me to actually do it. It's been an 'interesting' learning curve, but a totally enjoyable experience. I'm already well into book number two now – another travel memoir, based on a five-week backpacking adventure across India, in January 2020. See htps://www.mg-probert.com for the latest information. So, thank you to all those who launched my writing career.

I am hugely indebted to Helen Baggott and Kirstie Edwards for their editing and proofreading expertise. Somehow, they turned my 70,000 words into something readable. I thank them also for their professional approach and friendly encouragement. Proper writers and publishers, like Joanna Penn, Orna Ross, Dave Chesson, David Gaughran and Mark Dawson will never know how much inspiration they provided over the last couple of years. Tom Probert of www.tomprobert.design produced the fantastic book cover and maps, while Greg, Sarah and Nick provided crucial beta reader feedback and support.

Last, and very much top of the list – but held back for dramatic effect – the biggest thanks go to Jan, who still, after all these years, continues to put up with a wandering husband, who goes off and does silly things.

ABOUT MARK PROBERT

 Born in Hampshire in 1954, Mark Probert has spent most of his life as a mapmaker. After twenty eight years working for Ordnance Survey, he set up his own company in 2003 and spent the following seventeen years travelling extensively overseas. Now retired, and living in rural Shropshire, he spends his time writing, walking, cycling and motorcycling. That's when he isn't catching up with the domestic 'jobs list' his wife Jan has finally managed to give him. His second book, due in 2021, is another travel memoir that describes a coast to coast backpacking adventure across India. Mark traversed the subcontinent in January 2020 with his friend of 40 years, Nick Lindsay. Entrusted out on their own for five weeks, the boys narrowly avoided arrest on day one in an incident that set the tone for the rest of their adventure. Expect railways, curries, near-death road incidents, religious shrines, camels… and lots of cows.

ABOUT JOHN HILLABY

 When it comes to long-distance walking, John Hillaby wrote the book. In fact, he wrote several. Born in 1917, he became a journalist, an environmentalist and a prodigious walker. His first book, *Within the Stream*, was published in 1949, but his career as an author took off when he began a series of books about his exploits as a long-distance walker. *Journey through Britain* was published in 1968. He died in 1996.

His writing style is of its time, but always a pleasure to read. Accounts of his experiences are accompanied by well-researched information on the geography, archaeology, geology, and natural history of the areas through which he travelled. His books have a gentle pace that will soon have you in step with his walking. He had an eye for the quirky, and his writing demonstrates great subtlety and humour.

Journey through Britain is now out of print and the original publisher (Paladin) no longer exists. At the time of writing, however, used copies of the paperback can be obtained from online retailers.

Made in the USA
Columbia, SC
26 July 2021